Postcolonial Sovereignty?

Postcolonial Sovereignty?

The Nisga'a Final Agreement

◌

Tracie Lea Scott

PURICH
PUBLISHING
LIMITED
SASKATOON, SK. CANADA

Purich Publishing,
Box 23032, Market Mall Post Office, Saskatoon, SK, Canada, S7J 5H3
Phone: (306) 373-5311 Fax: (306) 373-5315 Email: purich@sasktel.net
www.purichpublishing.com

Library and Archives Canada Cataloguing in Publication

Scott, Tracie Lea, 1977 —
Postcolonial sovereignty? : the Nisga'a final agreement / Tracie Lea Scott.

Includes bibliographical references and index.
ISBN 978-1-895830-61-3

1. Nisga'a Nation. Treaties, etc. 1999 April 27. 2. Nis_ga'a Indians — Canada — Government relations. 3. Nis'ga'a Indians — British Columbia — Government relations. 4. Nis_ga'a Indians — British Columbia — Claims — History. 5. Nisga'a Indians — British Columbia — Land tenure — History. 6. Indian land transfers — British Columbia — History. I. Title.

KE7749.N5S36 2012   346.711'043208997412   C2011-908714-6
KF5662.N58S36 2012

Edited, designed, and typeset by Donald Ward, who also created the map.
Cover design by Jamie Olson.
Index by Ursula Acton.
Printed and bound in Canada at Houghton Boston Printers and Lithographers, Saskatoon.

Purich Publishing gratefully acknowledges the assistance of the Government of Canada through the Canada Book Fund (CBF), and the Creative Industry Growth and Sustainability Program made possible through funding provided to the Saskatchewan Arts Board by the Government of Saskatchewan through the Ministry of Tourism, Parks, Culture and Sport for its publishing program.

Printed on 100 per cent post-consumer, recycled, ancient-forest-friendly paper.

Canadian Patrimoine
Heritage canadien

SASKATCHEWAN
ARTS BOARD

Saskatchewan
Ministry of
Tourism, Parks,
Culture and Sport

Dedication

I think I can honestly say that nothing of great worth in this book is the result of my own creativity or intelligence. Indeed, if there is any value in the following chapters, it emerges from the patience, wisdom, tenacity, and ingenuity of the members of Nisga'a Nation, and all of the other Aboriginal scholars and activists who have been involved in the struggle for Aboriginal recognition and acceptance in Canada on just and equitable terms. Thus, while there is the usual cast of characters to whom I owe a great debt of gratitude — husband, family, supervisors, colleagues, and friends who have kindly supported and challenged me — I dedicate this book to the people who are truly responsible for the remarkable events that this book attempts to describe. I would like to dedicate this book to the Nisga'a Nation. I would also like to thank Don Purich, Karen Bolstad, and Don Ward who were responsible for guiding the transformation of a sufficient dissertation into a much better book.

Author's Note

I have used the spelling "postcolonial" throughout the book to refer generally to the theoretical school of thought. In the text, where "post-colonial" appears hypenated, it is used to refer to a time or phase after colonialism. I wished to avoid making the suggestion that we have presently reached this state of affairs when discussing the theoretical school.

There are two different versions of the Nisga'a Final Agreement available online. The references in this book are made to the pdf version online at www.aadnc-aandc.gc.ca/DAM/DAM-INTER-HQ/STAGING/texte-text/nis_1100100031253_eng.pdf, not the numbering found in the web version at www.aadnc-aandc.gc.ca/eng/1100100031252. When the book was being written, the most convenient online reference to the treaty was www.gov.bc.ca/arr/firstnation/nisgaa. This page is now a link to the official AADNC versions cited above.

Contents

○

Introduction

○

In 1969, when Jean Chrétien proposed the end of the *Indian Act* in the infamous White Paper, few Canadians expected the swift and passionate response that came from Aboriginal people across Canada. Even fewer anticipated that, less than fifty years later, rather than the demise of a distinct status for Aboriginal people, we would be witnessing the recognition of First Nation self-government as standard policy. In the pursuit of this policy, Canadian courts and politicians have been laying a path toward what the Supreme Court has described as the "reconciliation of the prior occupation of North America by distinctive aboriginal societies with the assertion of Crown sovereignty over Canadian territory. "[1] Some have observed that reconciliation, by necessity, requires that an essential quality of First Nation's independence must be abdicated, or reconciled, to the Canadian state.[2] Others have argued that recognition of First Nation self-government fundamentally compromises essential Canadian political values.[3] So, while we are laying a path, it seems far from clear where it leads. In this book, through examining the Nisga'a Final Agreement (NFA), one such comprehensive land claim and self-government agreement, I will explore where this path may take us, and how we may have to adjust our understandings of the law and sovereignty along this journey.

The main motivation for the dissertation that preceded this book was my fascination with the conflicting criticisms of the NFA. On one side of the political spectrum, commentators were announcing that the agreement was the beginning of the end of Western liberal democracy. On the other side, commentators were criticizing the agreement as yet another victory for Western colonial forces on the path to extinguishing Aboriginal rights once and for all. These conflicting critiques made me begin to wonder about how the agreement was seen by the people it affected the most — the Nisga'a. Indeed, at the first conference where I presented my idea for the dissertation, the first question I faced was how I could justify the fact that the Nisga'a had lost ninety per cent of the land they claimed by signing the agreement. As I had no answer, I thought I should ask the people who had negotiated and ultimately voted yes for the agreement in a referendum.

In the summers of 2005 and 2006, I travelled to the Nass Valley to ask some members of the Nisga'a Nation how the treaty had affected them. In semi-structured interviews, I asked various members of the Nisga'a Nation, as well as non-Nisga'a individuals who lived and worked in the communities, a set of open-ended question about the effect of the treaty:

1. One of the critiques offered about many of the modern agreements is that Aboriginal groups are still receiving only a small portion of their traditional lands. Is this a concern, and how would you respond to these peoples in regard to the Nisga'a treaty?

2. There seem to be provisions that allow the NFA to evolve in many different areas. Are there any particular areas that are priorities in this respect?

3. How has the implementation of the NFA and self-government changed the daily cultural, social, and economic circumstances for the Nisga'a?

4. The terms "self-determination" and "sovereignty" are bantered around a great deal by Aboriginal rights proponents and in the legal and academic literature. What does this mean for the Nisga'a Nation on a more practical level?

5. What effects has the implementation of the NFA had on relations with the Canadian and provincial governments?

6. What effects has the implementation of the NFA had on relations with local non-Aboriginal Canadians?

The conversations I had with both members of the Nisga'a Nation and non-members living in the community presented some challenges to the standard critiques in Aboriginal rights discourse. While the number of interviews was limited, these conversations were invaluable for informing the way I understood the treaty. I should emphasize, however, that this book in no way pretends to represent all the members of the Nisga'a Nation's views on the treaty.

Rather, it begins to present a picture of the more complex social and cultural factors that inform modern treaty making.

The first area where these interviews challenged a canonical interpretation of Aboriginal rights in Canada was in relation to land rights. Modern comprehensive treaties are regularly criticized for failing to recognize the true scope and extent of Aboriginal title. As mentioned earlier, the NFA has been criticized for recognizing only ten per cent of Nisga'a traditional lands. Members of the Nisga'a Nation who participated in the negotiation process, however, explained that, while the size of the land base was a compromise, the core Nisga'a lands they were granted was on terms that exceeded the usual understanding of Aboriginal title. Further, most of the remaining ninety per cent is subject to Nisga'a Aboriginal rights and co-management. As Peter Columbrander, assistant to the B. C. Treaty Commission, posited, rights and title claims in negotiations are being used as leverage for garnering governmental power. This approach to land title demonstrated that the real issue is not simply individual "ownership" in the traditional liberal sense, but rather a collective "ownership" in a governmental sense. An analysis of the NFA is, therefore, instructive as it demonstrates what the rough guidelines provided in *Delgamuukw* by the Supreme Court can mean in practice.

Traditional Aboriginal rights in the Nisga'a Final Agreement also raise some questions about typical institutional critiques of treaties. While Canadian jurisprudence has been uniformly criticized for conceptualizing Aboriginal rights as "frozen" in pre-contact cultural practices, there remains a discomfort with modern treaties that are more focused on current economic opportunities rather than traditional economies. The NFA, rather than securing the practice of traditional rights, instead uses these entitlements as a springboard to secure power over resources that are not circumscribed by a strict notion of traditional uses. The Nisga'a Nation, for example, was interested in developing sustainable commercial fisheries rather than merely securing continued individual fishing rights for members.

The NFA does not merely recognize Nisga'a title and traditional rights. The agreement recognized Nisga'a jurisdiction over land and resources. Indeed, it is the recognition of First Nation governance that has been the cause of most concern to some commentators, who felt that the NFA creates a racially based, third order of government. The NFA, while it secures access to resources, is not about rights. The NFA is fundamentally about power. This is the most important thing to recognize if we are going to ask how the NFA has affected Canadian law and society. The NFA is not about preserving Nisga'a culture as it existed before contact with outsiders; it is about the Nisga'a Nation taking its rightful place in contemporary Canada's political, economic, social, and cultural life.

How Far Have We Come?

While recounting some of the historical milestones since 1969 may be a familiar narrative to many, a review of Canadian-Aboriginal history demonstrates the necessity of a book such as this. A review of this history demonstrates how far down this path we have travelled, and how far we have to go. As Claude Denis has explained, Aboriginal people were facing an impossible catch-22 in the mid-twentieth century:

> From the arrival of Europeans in the Americas until the War of 1812 between the British Empire and the recently independent United States, Indigenous peoples were partners to the newcomers in what became Canada. They began as senior partners, becoming gradually equal and then increasingly subordinated. From at least the adoption of the *Indian Act* by the Canadian parliament in the late nineteenth century, and up until 1960, they were left with a difficult choice: on the one hand, they could maintain a devalued but meaningful Indian status and, on the other hand, they could abandon their Indigenous identities as the price for acquiring Canadian citizenship.[4]

Chrétien's answer to this predicament was to assimilate Aboriginal peoples into Canadian liberal democracy as individuals, equal before the law. This was not the vision of equality held by First Nations in Canada.

Rather swiftly after Chrétien announced the White Paper, Harold Cardinal released the book that has been called "The Red Paper."[5] This book was an exposé of the ignorance of Canadian society about the issues facing Aboriginal peoples in Canada and the denial of the government to address these issues in good faith. Cardinal's answer to this destructive politics was a call to action for Aboriginal peoples in Canada: "We will not trust the government with our futures any longer. Now they must listen to and learn from us."[6]

While Cardinal was helping to create a new radical politics, the courts were considering the legal status of First Nations. In 1967, Frank Calder of the Nisga'a Nation brought an application to the courts that Nisga'a Aboriginal title had never been extinguished. In 1973, the Supreme Court handed down a decision that demonstrated the deep legal ambivalence over the existence of Aboriginal land rights in Canada.[7] In this decision, the court split equally on the issue of whether Nisga'a title survived the unilateral assertion of crown sovereignty. Justices Martland, Judson, and Ritchie found that the governmental control exerted over Nisga'a lands was sufficient to extinguish Nisga'a claims by demonstrating inconsistency with continued Nisga'a sovereignty and title. Justices Hall, Spence, and Laskin, however, held that once an Aboriginal group proves Aboriginal title, appropriate surrender protocols must be followed in order to extinguish Aboriginal claims. They were of the view that the actions of the provincial governors in British Columbia were not consistent with these established protocols for surrender, and, therefore, not sufficient to extinguish Nisga'a title. Justice Pigeon, taking a different approach, was of the view that the Court did not even have jurisdiction to consider the question without a fiat from the Attorney General.

While the *Calder* decision was the first Supreme Court judgement to recognize pre-existing and continuing Aboriginal title, it was not a resounding victory for First Nations. The debate between the judgement penned by Hall and the one rendered by Judson was, in essence, about the extent of governmental action required to extinguish Nisga'a title. Even Hall, in dissent, does not state that Aboriginal title cannot be extinguished; he merely states that there were no actions taken that were sufficient to do so. In other words, in *Calder* we are still witness to the acceptable notion of the unprincipled unilateral extinguishment of Aboriginal title. It would take a steady procession of Aboriginal title cases in the Supreme Court to clarify the status of Aboriginal title in Canada. The *Delgamuukw*[8] decision, rendered in 1997, would eventually confirm that the unilateral assertion of Crown sovereignty is not an acceptable means of extinguishing Aboriginal title.

Calder was, therefore, only a first step toward the recognition of Aboriginal claims. The potential uncertainty created by the *Calder* decision compelled the government to reconsider the approach toward land where there was no clear historical surrender. In 1973, Jean Chrétien made a statement on the claims of Indian and Inuit people.[9] The aim of this initiative was "to obtain certainty respecting ownership, use and management of lands and resources by negotiating an exchange of claims to undefined Aboriginal rights for a clearly defined package of rights and benefits set out in a settlement agreement."[10] Negotiations for the repatriation of the constitution, however, created a much more ambitious program for First Nations governance. The recognition of "Aboriginal and Treaty Rights" in section 35 of the Constitution was followed by constitutionally mandated conferences to define these constitutionally entrenched rights. The focus, however, was not on rights as we may now think about them, but a much broader program — rights as expressed through Aboriginal self-government. In 1983, for example, the Standing Committee on Indian Affairs and Northern Development, chaired by Keith Penner, released their "Report of the Special Committee on Indian Self-Government."[11] This report recommended the recognition of First Nations governments as equivalent to provinces within the Canadian constitution. This report was initially met with general agreement. The political and constitutional discussions that followed the publication of this report continued this theme.

The constitutional conferences, however, came and went without leaving a profound mark on Canadian history. The political impetus for the implementation of First Nation self-government as envisioned in the Penner report waned when a Conservative government replaced the Liberals; with a new government came new approaches. In 1991, the Royal Commission on Aboriginal Peoples (RCAP) was established to examine the issues facing Aboriginal peoples in Canada. In 1992, the Charlottetown Accord, which included the recognition of Aboriginal self-government in principle among a raft of other proposals, failed to pass in a referendum. By 1996, when RCAP published its report, the Liberal party, lead by Jean Chrétien, once again gained a majority. This report also contained recommendations for Aboriginal self-government, which have not been implemented.

Despite the loss of a political will to address Aboriginal claims through a constitutional process, the legal processes marched on. In the *Delgamuukw* decision, a majority of the court recognized pre-existing Aboriginal title. The court also established guidelines for the extinguishment of Aboriginal title. Further, the court recognized oral history as a valid evidentiary source of occupation, therefore overcoming the nearly impossible evidentiary burden that had prevented recognition of pre-existing Aboriginal title. As E. Richard Atleo (Umeek), hereditary chief of the Nuu-Chah-nulth, writes,

> Towards the end of the twentieth century, paradigmatic changes had already begun for the Aboriginals of Canada. Through the lens of modernity, the Aboriginals were considered primitive and childlike. This attitude is reflected in the *Indian Act*. Aboriginal people and communities as self-governing entities with jurisdiction over their own sovereign territories were not recognized. The 1997 Supreme Court decision in *Delgamuukw* v. *British Columbia*, which made oral histories permissible

under Canadian law for the first time, is helping to change that. Aboriginal title to land, previously held in question, can now be recognized because of the *Delgamuukw* case. The hegemonic, one-world-order perspective of Canadian law has given way to the plurality of postmodernity by recognizing another perspective on land title.[12]

Since 1969 there has been a sea change in how the courts and the government have approached Aboriginal peoples in Canada. Chrétien's solution to the poverty and disadvantage of Aboriginal peoples was to apply an undifferentiated liberalism to the problem; if Indians were provided with strict formal equality, they would be raised from the disadvantage of their distinct status. The response to the White Paper, however, clearly demonstrated that Aboriginal peoples in Canada were not willing to sacrifice their Aboriginal national identities for a vision of traditional Western liberal equality.

Since 1973, twenty-two comprehensive land claims agreements have been ratified and brought into effect. These agreements negotiated the recognition of First Nations' right to land, resources, and self-determination with the assertion of Canadian sovereignty with varying levels of success in the eyes of critics. While the spectre of liberalism permeates these agreements, we are no longer in familiar territory. This book will delve into the implications of these agreements on Canadian legal and political culture through an examination of the Nisga'a Final Agreement.[13]

How Far We Have to Go

I argue that the Nisga'a Final Agreement represents a significant milestone in First Nation/Canadian relations. The treaty is a departure from a politics of formal liberal equality, and a movement toward a politics of differentiated citizenship. This book is an effort to understand how the treaty mediates between the liberal tenor of Canadian society and First Nation nationhood.

In chapter one, I argue that, with the treaty, we have reached the limits of liberal accommodation, and that a different analysis is now necessary. A liberal analysis cannot easily justify an ethnically constituted "third order" of government. I therefore argue that a postcolonial framework provides some insight into how we can understand First Nation governance in contemporary Canada. This chapter will explain how postcolonial theory is being invoked in relation to Aboriginal rights in Canada, and how it can lend to our understanding of how First Nation self-government can be understood within the Canadian constitution.

Through examining the land provision in the NFA in chapter two, I argue that a hybrid form of landholding is created that is neither traditionally Aboriginal nor Western. This analysis will demonstrate that the NFA creates a model of landholding that uses legal concepts familiar to the Canadian landholding system, yet implements characteristics of Aboriginal landholding fundamental to the ongoing survival of the Nisga'a Nation. This hybrid landholding created by the NFA creates legal uncertainty that generates anxiety about how the treaty will affect Canadian law and society.

Chapter three will further argue that the NFA provisions relating to resources implement a model that cannot be described as merely an accommodation within a liberal framework through examining other Aboriginal "rights" in the NFA. A liberal model recognizes rights as a fixed entitlement to certain historical practices. While not granting absolute power to the Nisga'a Nation in relation to resources (other than land), the NFA gives it recognized control over a broad scope of resources that are of both traditional and contemporary significance to the viability of the Nisga'a Nation. I argue that the NFA should be seen as defining the limitation of the sovereign authority of the Canadian state over the Nisga'a Nation. The NFA is a return to a nation-to-nation approach. The deep anxiety surrounding Aboriginal rights in the NFA is intimately tied to this concern over the limitation of the Canadian state's authority to govern without the Nisga'a Lisims Government's[14] participation.

Chapter four will more fully explore how the NFA implements Nisga'a Nation self-determination. It will examine how Nisga'a Nation governance is recognized in the treaty, and how this implements a model of Aboriginal governance that co-exists with Canadian sovereignty. This chapter will argue that this recognition (both legal and constitutional) allows the Nisga'a Nation to be a part of the Canadian political order and at the same time separate from it. This ambiguous positioning of the Nisga'a Nation will question the relevance of a traditional conception of sovereignty in an arrangement where the Nisga'a Nation has become a constitutionally recognized "nation" within the Canadian state. A traditional notion of "sovereignty," therefore, may be less relevant in the actual operation of the state.

Chapter five will explore how the NFA has been interpreted within Canadian law. This chapter will examine legal decisions that have challenged the validity of the NFA. These cases demonstrate that the NFA, by becoming a part of it, has become clothed with the same protection as the Canadian government and its sovereignty. Sovereignty is sometimes characterized as unchallengeable, and its source unquestionable. The *Campbell* case demonstrates, however, that the Canadian constitution can be interpreted as limiting the sovereign power of the state, rather than excluding Aboriginal sovereignty. The NFA, and the powers of the Nisga'a government within this interpretation, rather than being excluded by it, have been afforded the protection of Canadian sovereignty.

Chapter six will conclude that, if we understand sovereignty through the lens of nations and power, the NFA has many of the characteristics attributed to traditional notions of sovereignty. In Canadian legal and academic terminology, the concept of "self-determination" is deployed as a means to avoid the deeply held anxiety that First Nations have modified the "sovereignty" of the Canadian state. Through an analysis of the constituent powers of the NFA, self-determination does in fact represent a sharing of power that recasts the import of assertion of a unilateral, all-powerful sovereignty. I do not argue that Western conceptions of sovereignty do not have some discursive purchase. I will argue, however, that a paradigm shift to a postcolonial understanding of the contemporary nation state may be far more valuable in allowing the process of decolonization. A postcolonial understanding may indeed provide the analytical means to appreciate how we have moved beyond models of accommodation into a more inclusive and sometimes truly difficult postcolonial dynamic.

The NFA is a complex and multifaceted agreement. It may be generations before this treaty and its effects can be fully understood. What it does represent, however, is an answer to the many challenges Cardinal posed in *The Unjust Society*. In 1969 he wrote,

What the Indian wants is really quite simple. He wants the chance to develop the resources available to him on his own homeland, the reserve. What he needs to make this possible includes financial assistance, enough money to do the job properly so that he does not fail for lack of adequate financing; training in the precise skills he will need to develop the resources, training so practical and appropriate to the task that he will not fail because he does not have the know-how to do the job and, finally, access to expert advice and counsel throughout the stages of development so that he will not fail because he was given the wrong advice or no advice at all. With the money, the know-how and expert guidance, then if the Indian fails, at least it will not be because he didn't try to succeed and at least it will not be because he was not allowed to try.

One key factor remains, Indian involvement. Our people want the right to set their own goals, determine their own priorities, create and stimulate their own opportunities and development. The government knows this. This is part of what we have whispered, talked and screamed about. But the government mind, once on a path, seems difficult to divert. Once a government bureaucrat makes up his mind, there is no point trying to change it with logic and facts. And the government long ago decided it knew what was best for its Indian charges.[15]

The NFA does indeed recognize that the Nisga'a Nation has the power to decide its future place in the Canadian federation. The question now is whether the rest of Canada can accept the altered legal and political landscape that results from this recognition.

○

CHAPTER ONE

Postcolonial Sovereignty?

Introduction

The *Stanford Encyclopedia of Philosophy* observes, "[a]s soon as one examines it, 'liberalism' fractures into a variety of types and competing visions."[1] A brief survey of the writings on liberalism confirms that this may be one of the great understatements. The canon of "postcolonialism" is no less varied. While the main purpose of this book is to examine the Nisga'a Final Agreement and its effect on Canadian law and society, in light of the argument presented in the Introduction it will be necessary briefly to survey the species of liberalism and postcolonialism I am referring to when invoking these very broad theories. The criticisms of the treaty all implicitly draw on the values imbued in liberal discourse or critical theory. It is, therefore, crucial at least to attempt to delve into the primary insights in these theoretical notions in order to understand the critiques of the treaty.

In the Introduction, I argued that it is the powers granted in modern comprehensive treaties that cause the most anxiety. I suggested that the reason for this is that the recognition of ethnically based "third-order" governments present some fundamental challenges to cherished Canadian liberal values. It is therefore important to examine these values, and explore why First Nation self-government poses such difficulty to them. Luckily for me, this is by no means the first attempt to examine how a liberal democracy can simultaneously respect the mandate of equality while respecting cultural difference. Many Canadian academics have examined how multiculturalism can be harmonized with the values of liberal democracy.[2] In this book I will be using the work of political philosopher Will Kymlicka, author of *Liberalism, Community, and Culture*[3] and *Multicultural Citizenship: A Liberal Theory of Minority Rights*[4] to examine the rifts that emerge between liberalism and First Nation self-government. Kymlicka's exploration of the accommodation of multiculturalism in Canadian liberal democracy is particularly relevant because he directly addresses the distinction between First Nations and other ethnic minorities in Canada.

The second part of this chapter will attempt to draw out some general principles of postcolonial theory. While postcolonial theory can certainly be accused of not being the most straightforward theoretical writing, the basic ideas at the core of this theory have an immediate relevance to Aboriginal peoples in Canada. This is evident through even a cursory search of the term in Canadian legal journals. James Youngblood Henderson, among others, invokes the "postcolonial" as a means to describe the necessary movement away from a Western-dominated worldview to the recognition of Aboriginal culture as having equal value.[5]

While postcolonial theory is a rather heterogeneous body of theory, there are a few philosophers and literary critics who have been very influential in the development of the canon of postcolonialism. For the purpose of this book, I will be mainly referring to Homi Bhabha, Edward Said, and Michel Foucault. Homi Bhabha is probably best known for his book *The Location of Culture*.[6] It is in this work, and others, that he develops some of the main concepts central to postcolonial thought: hybridity, difference, and ambivalence, to name a few. Edward Said is one of the founders of postcolonialism through his examination of colonial discourse in *Orientalism*.[7] Finally, there are some references to the theory of discourse found in the work of Michel Foucault, whose ideas on language and discourse form a conceptual background to both Bhabha and Said. To briefly map how these ideas are important in this book: Foucault provides a way to look at the productive life of language, Said applies this idea of the productivity of language to colonial relationships, and Bhabha argues that this productivity is a two-way street with unique cultural outcomes.

A Very Canadian Liberalism

The argument I will develop in this book is that the recognition of First Nations as a part of Canada's political and constitutional structure has created anxiety with regard to contemporary treaties. These agreements represent a challenge to the liberal values of governance to which Canadians have a deep attachment. Even with the recognition of Aboriginal rights in section 35 of the Constitution, First Nation self-government is difficult to account for, even with a modified liberalism. As we reach the limits of a liberal analysis, we need to look for new ways to understand the Canadian political and constitutional arrangement. I argue that modern comprehensive treaties should instead be seen as the development of a postcolonial sovereignty — a sovereignty that recognizes multiple sources of legal and governmental authority and legitimacy.

Liberalism, however, is the subject of continual debate. As such, while again presenting a familiar discussion, I am going to use the work of Will Kymlicka as representative of a very Canadian breed of liberal values to tease out a workable core definition of liberalism.

There are several reasons why Kymlicka's work is a particularly appropriate example of liberal theory in relation to this project. The first is that he provides a relatively "stripped down" version of basic liberal principles. This simplicity avoids the more thorny political debates around the meaning of autonomy and its components within liberal discourse.

This simplicity arises from the fairly straightforward enunciation of the concept of autonomy. In *Liberalism, Community and Culture*, Kymlicka describes the political morality of contemporary liberalism:

> So we have two preconditions for the fulfillment of our essential interest in leading a life that is good. One is that we lead our lives from the inside, in accordance with our beliefs about what gives value to life; the other is that we be free to question those beliefs, to examine them in light of whatever information and examples and arguments our culture can provide. Individuals must therefore have the resources and liberties needed to live their lives in accordance with their beliefs about value, without being imprisoned or penalized for unorthodox religious or sexual practices etc.[8]

Liberal autonomy requires that individuals are allowed to live according to their core fundamental principles, and that they are allowed to revise these beliefs when desired. This description of what autonomy requires avoids the moral and functional justifications of liberal values by extolling (and debating) the functional and moral components (and benefits) of autonomy. Kymlicka's version of liberalism, therefore, avoids some of the normative liberal philosophical debate better left to political scientists.

Liberalism and Culture

Kymlicka's engagement with liberal theory and minority cultures is premised upon rethinking the importance of culture in liberal theory. A primary motivation for the writing of *Liberalism, Community and Culture*, as stated in the introduction, is his "discomfort with recent communitarian discussions of culture and community"[9] that underestimate liberalism's ability to account for the "individual's membership in a community and culture."[10] This revaluation of the importance of culture in liberalism then, in turn, supports his argument that culture is an important enough factor to justify the accommodation of minority cultural rights. If we refer to the "preconditions for the fulfillment of our essential interest in leading a life that is good,"[11] we must have the ability to live our lives according to the values we hold, and the freedom to review these values according to the choices presented to us. Kymlicka's most unadorned, yet insightful, addition to liberal theory, therefore, is to identify the importance of culture to the fulfillment of these essential preconditions. Indeed, he argues that culture is such a fundamental factor in one's personal value system and ability to make choices that it is a necessary context for the all-important concept of liberal autonomy. The consequences of this insight, however, are not so straightforward.

While *Liberalism, Community and Culture* was devoted to identifying the capacity of liberalism to account for community and culture, the argument that this recognition normatively justifies the accommodation of minority rights within certain liberal limits is argued more fully in Kymlicka's following book, *Multicultural Citizenship: A Liberal Theory of Minority Rights*. In *Liberalism*, Kymlicka identified some of the "political challenges"[12] posed by minorities such as French-Canadians and Aboriginal peoples. It is in *Multicultural Citizenship*, however, that this theory of minority rights is more fully articulated.

The logical integrity of Kymlicka's ideas about liberal accommodation presented in *Multicultural Citizenship* rests on the distinction between different species of minority rights, for each species has an independent normative logic. He identifies three categories of rights relevant to his argument for the accommodation of minority rights: national minority rights, polyethnic rights, and special rights. National minorities are defined as a minority population that comprise a "nation." A nation, according to Kymlicka's definition, "means a historical community, more or less institutionally complete, occupying a given territory or homeland, sharing a distinct language and culture."[13]

The larger political organization — what Kymlicka terms the "multinational state" — is the state that has incorporated these smaller nations into a larger political unit by conquest, colonization, or choice. The rights involved with the claims of national minorities are some form of self-government rights, described by Kymlicka as claims that

> typically take the form of devolving political power to a political unit substantially controlled by the members of the national minority, and substantially corresponding to their historical homeland or territory. It is important to note that these claims are not seen as a temporary measure, nor as a remedy for a form of oppression that we might (and ought) someday to eliminate. On the contrary, these rights are often described as "inherent," and so permanent (which is one reason why national minorities seek to have them entrenched in the constitution).[14]

The second category is polyethnic rights, which are rights of minorities "intended to help ethnic groups and religious minorities express their cultural particularity and pride without hampering their success in the economic and political institutions of the dominant society."[15] The third group Kymlicka identifies is special representation rights. This rather nebulous category is a rather different species of right, aimed at countering the lack of democratic representation of members of under-represented groups such as ethnic minorities, women, or disabled individuals.

Only the category of multinational rights shall be dealt with in any detail, with some discussion of the other species for comparison only. The reason for this is that Aboriginal peoples in Canada fall clearly under this category, as they were previously sovereign[16] groups incorporated through colonization. It is this history of colonization that underlies one of Kymlicka's strongest arguments for national minority rights for Aboriginal peoples.

Polyethnic rights recognize that groups such as immigrants may be adversely affected by the dominance of one cultural group in a liberal democracy, thus necessitating some accommodation so as to not be disadvantaged in society. This is a matter of equality. These groups, according to Kymlicka, require positive steps to protect them against discrimination, not rights of self-determination. Indeed, these rights "are usually intended to promote integration into the larger society."[17] Examples given of this type of right include "Jews and Muslims in Britain [who] have sought exemption from Sunday closing or animal slaughtering legislation; Sikh men in Canada [who] have sought exemption from motorcycle helmet laws and from the official dress-code of police forces, so they can wear their turban."[18] Groups such as these are generally disadvantaged because their practices or customs do not align with the dominant society's. Measures that accommodate these groups are taken so that they do not suffer a disadvantage.

While the equality argument for polyethnic rights would potentially serve to support a great many positive actions to maintain Aboriginal cultural activities and language, for example, this argument is limited in its scope. The equality argument can only justify special accommodation until the group is no longer disadvantaged. Once the minority group enjoys the same benefits as the majority group, special measures are no longer warranted. As Kymlicka explains, "[t]his equality-based argument will only endorse special rights for national minorities if there actually is a disadvantage with respect to cultural membership, and if the rights actually serve to rectify the disadvantage."[19] Equality is, therefore, a great argument to support minority rights until an equilibrium is reached. At this point, "demands for increased powers of resources will not be necessary to ensure the same opportunity to live and work in one's culture. Instead, they will simply be attempts to gain benefits denied to others, to have more resources to pursue one's way of life than to others."[20] In relation to Aboriginal land rights, for example, "[o]ne could imagine a point where the amount of land reserved for indigenous peoples would not be necessary to provide reasonable external protections, but would rather provide unequal opportunities to them."[21]

This normative justification for accommodation thus falls short in justifying Aboriginal land claims and self-government agreements, as it would only justify positive support for a limited amount of time if there were an actual disadvantage within dominant society, and only for a limited scope of activities to correct this disadvantage. If we examine this logic, we are still squarely within the parameters of liberal rationality, and not in any significant way seeing the revision of fundamental liberal principles through Aboriginal perspectives. Indeed, the Nisga'a, for example, are in their estimation entitled to their land because of their long historical, social, and spiritual connection to it. The treaty is not predicated on an exercise of ensuring equality of resources with non-Nisga'a peoples.

The equality justification may fall short of supporting ongoing self-government rights; however, in *Multicultural Citizenship*, Kymlicka presents further rationales for national minority rights. National minorities are given a different status based on several distinct differences. The primary difference that Kymlicka sees between immigrant communities of, for example Sikhs, and Aboriginal peoples is a concept that he calls "societal culture." A societal culture is one "whose practices and institutions cover the full range of human activities, encompassing both public and private life."[22] An immigrant, according to this argument, left his or her institutional, bureaucratic, and social groupings behind in their home country and are thus not entitled to group rights. Kymlicka is of the opinion that "they bring with them a 'shared vocabulary of tradition and convention' [but] they have uprooted themselves from the social practices which this vocabulary originally referred to and made sense of."[23] Aboriginal people have not uprooted themselves by leaving their culture, institutions, and land, but rather, colonizers imposed a new set of institutions, laws, and social norms on them. We see the liberal notion of choice rearing its head as an important part of the justification of national minority rights. This difference gives rise to another important normative justification for national minority rights — historical agreements.

Beyond a simple equality argument, then, there is a more important justification in relation to Aboriginal-Canadian relations. This normative justification for differential rights is what Kymlicka describes as the "role of historical agreements."[24] The basic argument is that "the way a national minority was incorporated often gives rise to certain group-differentiated rights."[25] This justification simply recognizes the importance of honouring agreements made when the national minority was being incorporated into the federation. The difference between the equality argument and the historical argument is great, as it necessitates a different approach toward minority groups. As Kymlicka writes,

> While the equality and historical arguments often lead to the same result, they are none the less quite distinct. On the historical argument, the question is not how should the state treat "its" minorities, but rather what are the terms under which two or more peoples decided to become partners? The question is not how should the state act fairly in governing its minorities, but what are the limits to the state's right to govern them?[26]

The terms of the question are rather different. Instead of asking what allowances or positive steps the dominant society should take, the question becomes, what limits are there to the imposition of the dominant colonial society's rules?

In Canadian jurisprudence, considering the "rights" of Aboriginal peoples in their historical contexts has been the billion-dollar question. Many Aboriginal rights, including land, were historically denied to Aboriginal peoples through the government and the courts' assertion of the dominance of Crown sovereignty claims over Aboriginal claims. In other words, it was assumed that European settlement gave the new colonial political government the right to govern Aboriginal groups with impunity, and discount any previous political and legal arrangement. For example, in the *St. Catherine's Milling* case,[27] Aboriginal title was characterized as merely a "personal and usufructary right dependent on the goodwill of the Sovereign."[28] Colonization, in this characterization, meant the extinguishment of any Aboriginal rights except for ones that the Crown had the good nature to bestow upon his or her Indian subjects.

At the Limits of Liberalism

Over a hundred years later, we have a new legal and constitutional situation. The entrenchment of Aboriginal rights in the *Canadian Charter of Rights and Freedoms* (Part I of the *Constitution Act, 1982*) in section 25, and the *Constitution Act* (Part II)[29] in section 35 created new constitutional considerations. This section guarantees any rights garnered through treaty or through the historical declaration.[30] This provision, therefore, acts to shield Aboriginal peoples from the "ordinary" operation of the Charter that might compromise their distinct historical position through other Charter rights such as "equality." Section 35, integrated into the main body of the *Constitution* rather than the *Charter of Rights and Freedoms*, states that "the existing aboriginal and treaty rights of the aboriginal peoples of Canada are hereby recognized and affirmed."[31] Section 35.1 also guarantees Aboriginal representation in any discussions about changes to sections that apply to Aboriginal peoples in the Constitution.

These constitutional provisions, not surprisingly, have become the standard from which Aboriginal rights are now being determined. Indeed, section 35 caused the redefinition of the judicial test for Aboriginal rights in Canada. These cases, however, though demonstrating the logic of the liberal argument for accommodation due to historical relationships, do not demonstrate a profound shift away from the logic of colonial administration. For example, in 1996, the Supreme Court heard the case of Dorothy Marie Van der Peet.[32] She had sold ten salmon that were caught under an Indian food licence that prohibited the commercial sale of fish that were caught pursuant to this type of license. In her defence, Van der Peet alleged that she and the other members of the Sto:lo nation had a right to fish commercially pursuant to the rights guaranteed under section 35 — the Sto:lo's unextinguished right to continue the traditional pre-contact practice of fishing to participate in a market of exchange. Any limitation of this right, she alleged, violated the constitutionally protected rights of the Sto:lo.

The court in its definition of an Aboriginal rights, however, decided that the characterization of an Aboriginal right must be done with the purpose of section 35 in mind. This purpose, according to the majority of the court,

> is the reconciliation of the pre-existence of distinctive aboriginal societies with the assertion of Crown sovereignty. Courts adjudicating aboriginal rights claims must, therefore, be sensitive to the aboriginal perspective, but they must also be aware that aboriginal rights exist within the general legal system of Canada.[33]

This reconciliation requires the court to consider an "aboriginal perspective while at the same time taking into account the perspective of the common law."[34] More importantly, though, according to the majority, Aboriginal rights must reflect the logic of recognition which is premised on recognizing "the fact that prior to the arrival of Europeans in North America the land was already occupied by distinctive aboriginal societies, and as, second, the means by which that prior occupation is reconciled with the assertion of Crown sovereignty over Canadian territory."[35] It is this logic of pre-existence *and* reconciliation that supports the court's use of the standard that an Aboriginal right must be an integral cultural practice that "must be of central significance to the aboriginal society in question."[36] In the court's opinion, recognizing rights that were central to the Aboriginal society before European settlement satisfies the aspect of pre-existence and recognizes the span of years where the Crown has been sovereign. Thus, to satisfy this test, the practice must be distinctive, central, and pre-exist European interference. In this case, the court decided that the Sto:lo failed to prove that commercial fishing was central to their culture prior to contact with Europeans.[37] While prior to contact, the Sto:lo may not have exchanged fish for money, it is difficult to presume that the Sto:lo had never exchanged their catch for other goods. This would be loosely analogous to saying that our modern form of economy (capitalism) is not an integral part of our culture. If this were the case, then the Cold War, or other struggles over small and insignificant things such as economic ideology, ought not to have happened.

This decision, almost uniformly criticized by Aboriginal rights proponents for merely replicating "European paternalism,"[38] is a rule that defies sensible determination. The determination of cultural centrality in this manner ignores, as Henderson and Barsh argue, three basic realities. First, it is absurd that this determination be left to the trier of fact, as one cannot objectively determine the importance of a cultural activity to another person or group.[39] Second, this determination assumes that each cultural practice can be isolated from others like small, self-contained water jars.[40] Culture is not simply a list of independent practices that can be isolated from one another. Third, not recognizing the dynamism of any cultural practice is also absurd.[41] This logic is both replicating Eurocentric assumptions of Aboriginal cultures and simplifying the notion of culture to the point of ridiculousness. This test does, however, take into account the historical manner of incorporation. As this case demonstrates, the liberal recognition of the manner of historical incorporation is not sufficient to guarantee that the pre-existing practices of First Nations will be protected — after all, the goal must be the reconciliation of Aboriginal peoples with the sovereignty of Canada. Thus, while we see an overt acceptance of Aboriginal peoples' perspective, there is still a clear prioritizing of the sovereignty of Canada.

Aside from these fairly common criticisms,[42] however, I would suggest there is another way to evaluate the result of the case. In Kymlicka's account of liberal accommodation, he accepts that Aboriginal groups may have differential rights based on the manner of historical incorporation. In the case of the Nisga'a Final Agreement, the negotiation between the Nisga'a and the federal and provincial governments was not about just about rights, but about power. To provide an example, in the treaty, "subject to Nisga'a laws, Nisga'a citizens have the right to trade or barter among themselves or with other aboriginal people any fish or aquatic plants harvested in Nisga'a fisheries."[43] This was a provision agreed on by the Nisga'a, the federal government, and the provincial government, not simply a right determined by a court. Even more remarkably, though, the "Nisga'a fish entitlements are held by the Nisga'a Nation,"[44] and do not require "federal or provincial licenses,"[45] and are not subject to "fees, charges, or royalties."[46] This is not to say that the Nisga'a have unlimited entitlement to fish and other aquatic animals, but they do have a measure of control over what they are entitled to.

Even at a cursory glance, the provisions of the treaty are far more favourable than the Supreme Court's definition of Sto:lo fishing rights. As Peter Columbrander, assistant to the B.C. Treaty Commission, commented, in the treaty negotiation process, rights are best used as a bargaining tool for gaining power.[47] In an extended discussion about the NFA and the role of the Commission, he expressed the thought that the success of treaty negotiations for the First Nation was dependent on the Nation striking a balance between rights and power. In the *Van der Peet* case, the determination of the rights of the Sto:lo was in the power of the Supreme Court, bound by rhetoric about "reconciling rights with the sovereignty of Canada." This process, and consequentially this result, is not a "fully achieved postcolonial" conclusion. Thus, while we see the postcolonial influence of Aboriginal people within legal discourse, it is ultimately frustrated by a liberally constituted court that claims the right of deliberation over Aboriginal culture.

As resistant to logic as the *Van der Peet* case is, it was about fishing rights. A later case, *Pamajewon*,[48] demonstrates an even more striking colonial resilience in the face of Aboriginal "rights" claims in a context that is even more imperative. In the *Pamajewon* case, several members of the Shawanaga First Nation and the Eagle Lake First Nation were charged with *Criminal Code*[49] violations for the keeping of a common gaming house. The Shawanaga First Nation alleged that these *Criminal Code* violations were of no force and effect, as they had the inherent right to self-government pursuant to section 35 of the *Constitution*. The Eagle Lake First Nation, a little less ambitiously, claimed the right to regulate economic activities pursuant to the same Constitutional section. The claims made on behalf of the respective Nations are claims of self-determination or an inherent independence from the Canadian *Criminal Code* in these matters. The court, when faced with this problem of determining the validity of applying Canadian criminal law to First Nations, decided that

> The appellants' claim involves the assertion that s. 35(1) encompasses the right of self-government, and that this right includes the right to regulate gambling activities on the reservation. Assuming without deciding that s. 35(1) includes self-government claims, the applicable legal standard is nonetheless that laid out in *Van der Peet, supra.* Assuming s. 35(1) encompasses claims to aboriginal self-government, such claims must be considered in light of the purposes underlying that provision and must, therefore, be considered against the test derived from consideration of

those purposes. This is the test laid out in *Van der Peet, supra.* In so far as they can be made under s. 35(1), claims to self-government are no different from other claims to the enjoyment of aboriginal rights and must, as such, be measured against the same standard.[50]

The right to inherent self-government is then judged by the "integral to a distinctive culture test."[51] Additionally, as it is a question of rights, the scope of the right must be "looked at in light of the specific circumstances of each case and, in light of the specific history and culture of the aboriginal group claiming the right."[52] This required level of specificity resulted in the judge concluding that these First Nations were not alleging a right to self-government, but a right to regulate high-stakes gambling.

The conclusion is fairly self-evident. Sufficient evidence was not presented to draw the conclusion that "large-scale [gambling] activities"[53] and regulation of such was integral to the distinctive culture of the Ojibwa. Indeed, Chief Justice Lamer quotes from the Provincial Court decision in the case of *Gardener* that "[c]ommercial lotteries such as bingo are a twentieth century phenomenon and nothing of the kind existed amongst aboriginal peoples and was never part of the means by which those societies traditionally sustained or socialized."[54] This was apparently a right that, by its characterization, could never have been a pre-existing inherent right, and thus could never have passed the *Van der Peet* test. High stakes gambling is the product of such a transformation, and represents an important contemporary method of economic gain (or, to be more blunt, a means of escaping crushing poverty) for many First Nations.[55] The court, however, is unwilling to authorize an Aboriginal right over an area that is not simply a historical anachronism but a relevant contemporary industry.

While the "historical agreement" normative rationale has its limitations, Kymlicka offers another that supports assertions of independent Aboriginal governmental existence. This rationale is the "analogy with other states" argument. This justification is based on the limitations liberal states put on members within their own organizations. If liberal states maintain the power to limit citizenship in their political communities, then why are they hostile to accepting that an internal cultural group should have group-differentiated rights? If being a Canadian citizen allows one access to special benefits in Canada, while being Somali or American without the appropriate immigration status does not, there is a discontinuity with liberal discourse that frowns upon internally differentiated rights. At the very least, this claim supports, as

Kymlicka writes, a shift in the burden of proof. He concludes,

> In so far as liberal theorists accept the principle that citizenship can be restricted to members of a particular group, the burden of proof lies on them to explain why they are not also committed to accepting group-differentiated rights within the state. So long as liberals believe in separate states with restricted citizenship, the burden of proof lies as much with the opponents of group-differentiated rights as with their defenders.[56]

So, if equality is truly the order of the day, then there must be some discussion as to why the liberal state is allowed to restrict membership, while national minorities within the liberal state can be denied it.

In Aboriginal communities, this is an important and much-debated issue. The *Manitoba Act, 1870*[57] that established the province of Manitoba, for example, was initially created to pacify (otherwise described as incorporate) the Native population after the Red River Rebellion (otherwise known as the Red River Settlement) of 1869. Without control of membership, however, the continuous settlement of the area by Europeans ultimately undermined this political configuration as an expression of Native goals. In democracy, after all, the majority does rule. This same debate was held during talks leading to the creation of Nunavut on April 1, 1999. The Inuit of Nunavut, however, aware of the dangers a democratic government posed to Indigenous priority, still opted for a public government. It is unlikely in Nunavut, however, being located in one of the least habitable climates on earth, that a rash of European settlement poses as much of an imminent threat. Thus, control of membership within a democratic formulation of government can be an essential tool for the continuation of Aboriginal culture.

The final justification Kymlicka provides for accommodating national minority rights is the "value of cultural diversity" argument. While he dismisses this argument as unable to logically rationalize justifying specific national minority rights, he does recognize that this type of argument can bolster group-differentiated claims in a "quasi-aesthetic sense that creates a more interesting world [as] other cultures contain alternative models of social organization that may be useful in adapting to new circumstances."[58] This argument, as noted in Kymlicka and expanded in Macklem, is limited in its ability to support national minority rights, however, as it would place Aboriginal peoples in the same category as other minorities. The main problem, succinctly stated, is that this rationale gives the same normative support for claims to immigrant groups as it does to First Nations. This conflation is dangerous, as it ignores the other historical differences Aboriginal claims are based on.[59]

In relation to Aboriginal peoples, then, we have several normative arguments for why a liberal system should accommodate national minorities with some form of claim to self-determination or governance. The first, and not so persuasive, is the equality argument. This argument can only justify the positive support of the national minority's culture by funding limited activities. The equality argument cannot justify this accommodation for any longer than it takes to address the actual disadvantage. The role of historical agreements is a much stronger justification for the creation of Aboriginal self-government. The general argument that the way a people were incorporated, or "colonized," can give rise to much broader rights as agreed in treaty or other understanding has a greater potential. The application of similar principles in Canadian Aboriginal rights jurisprudence, however, has proven to be limited by the assertion of Crown sovereignty, despite the manner of historical incorporation. Another normative justification Kymlicka makes that pertains to national minorities is the "analogy with states" argument. This is a rather interesting and clever argument for its implications. If a state has the inviolable right to control citizenship, than there needs to be some justification for denying an analogous group such rights. If the historical agreement justification is limited by Crown sovereignty, however, it seems unlikely that this shift in the burden of proof would have more weight in the hallowed halls of colonial power. Finally, we have seen the argument that cultural diversity is valuable. This argument, if taken as a serious argument rather than a generally accepted platitude, jeopardizes Aboriginal claims, as they need to be differentiated from other minority groups.

Thus far, we have seen that Kymlicka has constructed normative justifications within liberal theory that attempt to harmonize national minority claims for rights such as self-determination through an equality argument, a historical argument, an analogy to other states, and the value of diversity claim. The equality argument, as the earlier discussion of the turban issue demonstrates, is a familiar logic in the determination of discrimination claims under s. 15 of the *Charter*. Substantive equality has become an enshrined principle in *Charter* jurisprudence. Aboriginal rights, however, are not a matter of simple discrimination. The most applicable normative justification is that of historical claims, whereby the manner in which a national minority was incorporated can give rise to differential group treatment. In Aboriginal rights jurisprudence, this argument has been highly influential in the recognition of Aboriginal claims. Aboriginal land claims, for example, have been validated under the argument that they had pre-existing, continuous, and unextinguished occupation of the land from the time prior to European settlement to the present.[60] Other Aboriginal rights, such as hunting and fishing, have been supported through historical treaties, where there were treaties signed, or by the existence of an unextinguished right that has been continuously exercised from pre-contact to the present.[61]

Kymlicka's normative justification for accepting Aboriginal claims to both rights and self-government may be familiar to the logic employed by the Canadian Supreme Court; however, this harmony has not lessened the criticism of his theory from both supporters of a more "pure" liberal stance and Aboriginal self-government. The critique from the liberalists has been fairly predictable — that entrenching group rights in any form compromises a truly liberal stance. As one commentator concludes, "As a liberal theory Kymlicka's conception of minority rights becomes incoherent as it relies upon false principles to supply a protection that is at best unnecessary, and at worst antagonistic to his aims of liberal equality."[62]

It is the critiques from supporters of Aboriginal claims that are far more interesting. There are two important critiques that, while connected, have different dimensions. After the publication of *Liberalism*, Patrick Macklem, a Canadian constitutional academic, wrote a rejoinder critiquing group rights based on the equality justification. The point Macklem makes is that, if Aboriginal groups are to get self-government based on an equality argument, they will never be able to transcend the sovereign grip of the colonial power they wish to be independent from:

> Kymlicka's work is a sophisticated and subtle attempt to ascribe moral status to cultural membership within the confines of liberal political theory. Nonetheless, Kymlicka's initial characterization of the problem indelibly marks his conclusion. By viewing the moral or political issue implicated by indigenous difference as one that requires justification of unequal distribution of political rights and responsibilities within a particular nation-state, Kymlicka includes indigenous people in the very political structure from which they seek a measure of autonomy.[63]

Thus, we see one critique of Kymlicka's equality argument: the inability of any Aboriginal self-government created and justified by a liberal system to allow the possibility for "independent action"[64] harmonious with their cultural values that may not be with the values of the liberal nation-state.

The equality argument is not the only justification Kymlicka presents in *Multicultural Citizenship*. In this book, Kymlicka develops the alternative basis for supporting national minority rights, including the value of cultural diversity, the analogy with states, and the historical agreement justification. It is through exploring the historical agreement justification that we can further interrogate the limitation in a liberal recognition of Aboriginal self-government. This argument, described by Spaulding as the modified equality argument, theoretically allows for a much broader recognition of Aboriginal rights and governance. If a group is in a treaty relationship, rather than simply being another minority, the treaty can authorize rights and powers that are not justified by an equality argument. This is so for two reasons. First, the equality argument only justifies differential group treatment while there is an actual disadvantage. What happens when there is no longer a manifest disadvantage? The differential treatment is no longer justifiable. Would Aboriginal governance rights then be revoked? A treaty, however, creates a basis for continuing self-government. Second, the equality argument only authorizes differential treatment that aligns with the goals of equality. Most historical treaties include fairly broad and unrestricted rights to marine or animal resources. A right such as this already far surpasses the ordinary rights of other citizens. Unless one can sustain an argument that this right is required to fix a manifest disadvantage, these rights are unsupportable with the equality argument. In this example, however, one could even argue that continuing "backwards activities" such as Aboriginal hunter-gatherer practices is what disadvantages them. These arguments are thus not only dangerous for the continuance of Aboriginal cultures, but also leave the determination of what rights are necessary within the power of the dominant groups that colonized Aboriginal peoples in the first place. This is hardly a move beyond the grip of colonialism.

The historical agreement rationale, then, allows for the historical anomalies that are already manifest in the Canadian political community. Unfortunately, even this rationale is limited in Kymlicka's account. The primary limitation is that the historical agreement must still dovetail with the equality argument. As Kymlicka writes, "the historical and equality arguments must work together."[65] While he agrees that national minorities should have some level of autonomy if the circumstances warrant it, there are fundamental limitations required to "ground the historical agreements in a deeper theory of justice."[66]

This is because ultimately a liberal theory of minority accommodation still must, at its core, maintain liberal values. Thus, "toleration [has] its limits."[67] The limits that Kymlicka sees as essential to maintaining the ability to lead one's life according to one's values, and have the freedom to revise one's values, is his expression of the core of liberal principles. Kymlicka, then, believes that the limitations that must be put on multicultural accommodation is to allow external protections, but limit internal restrictions. As Kymlicka writes,

> A liberal worldview requires freedom within the minority group and equality between the minority and majority groups. A system of minority rights which respects these two limitations is, I believe, impeccably liberal. It is consistent with, and indeed promotes, basic liberal values.[68]

If we take this restriction into account, then a historical agreement that guarantees a group any right that is inconsistent with these values is not justified. A national minority, then, may have some level of autonomy from the majority culture, but only if it is consistent with the values of the liberal majority culture. This can hardly be said to transcend the paternalistic and ethnocentric history of colonialism.

In Kymlicka's defence, though, it cannot be said that the potential maintenance of ethnocentric and colonial practices in his theory goes without comment and consideration. Kymlicka is not stating that his impeccably liberal system ought to be imposed. Indeed, he admits that

> Liberals have no automatic right to impose their views on non-liberal national minorities. But they do have the right, and indeed the responsibility, to identify what those views actually are. Relations between national groups should be determined by dialogue. But if liberal theory is to contribute anything to that dialogue, it is surely by spelling out the implications of the liberal principles of freedom and equality. That is not the first step down a path of interference. Rather, it is the first step in starting a dialogue.[69]

Kymlicka, then, is not ultimately advocating that his theory ought to be imposed on national minorities, limitations and all. He is really only discussing principles within liberal discourse and how liberal theory should view cultural membership. He recognizes that there is no right to impose liberalism on members of groups that are not liberal. It is my assertion, though, that even viewing cultural membership rights this way constricts the potential of a realized post-colonial state.

While Kymlicka's version of liberal theory is progressive and influential in Canadian discourse, it cannot account fully for the division of sovereignty into ethnically defined national minority groups. Aboriginal self-government still presents the possibility of illiberal effects that are not justifiable under liberal accommodation. And if we do use this model, we end up limiting the possibilities of action open to an internal national minority, and possibly excluding their existence entirely.

While liberal accommodation presents an attractive argument, it does not solve the problem of how different (illiberal) group values can be accounted for within a liberal system. Kymlicka does suggest the way to address this problem — through "starting a dialogue." Initiating this process may indeed lead to a way to elide the seemingly irreconcilable differences between liberal theory and Aboriginal rights. Turner has argued that Kymlicka's rationalization of Aboriginal rights ultimately fails because it does not allow the space for Aboriginal peoples to engage in the dialogue. He concludes:

> Kymlicka's liberalism does not require the participation of Aboriginal peoples in order to determine the content of their "special rights." This is because Aboriginal rights are justified within a distributive theory of justice that does not fully recognize the legitimacy of Aboriginal sovereignty. Many Aboriginal people contend that their rights of governance flow from their political sovereignty and that these rights ought to be recognized by the Canadian governments. . . . However, to do so in a just way requires a re-examination of Aboriginal incorporation between Aboriginal peoples and the Canadian state. The meaning of Aboriginal incorporation is problematic because Aboriginal interpretations have not been recognized by the dominant colonial governments; therefore, it matters how we go about understanding its meaning.[70]

Modern treaty negotiation is indeed the process that allows Indigenous participation and deliberation in a meaningful way.

Postcolonial Sovereignty?

The Nisga'a Final Agreement presents challenges to a liberal conception of political community. A treaty such as the NFA that allows for the sharing of sovereign authority in the form of self-government can be interpreted as a threat to a liberal formulation of society. In this section, the foundation for an alternative analysis will be elaborated through exploring postcolonial theory and some of its insights. Postcolonial theory is a term that describes a wide variety of approaches and critical concerns. The analysis presented here will mainly rely on Homi Bhabha's formulation of the postcolonial, although reference to the work of Edward Said and Michel Foucault are also inevitable as they form a conceptual background to Bhabha's work.

A basic description of postcolonial theory begins with the one notion that all postcolonial theory shares — a general concern with the interrelation between colonized peoples and the rest of the world. This, however, is where the reasonably uncontestable unities end. Drawing from post-structuralism, psychoanalysis, and literary criticism, postcolonial theory contains varied theoretical approaches.

Many of the core ideas of postcolonial theory arise from Bhabha's book, *The Location of Culture*. While this work is mainly concerned with the British experience in India, there are several insights that are applicable to all legal and political relationships. First, Bhabha approaches language in a particular way. Rather than characterizing language, or discourse, as a passive reflection of the world, he conceives of language as an active force in creating the world. Discourse does not just reproduce history; it creates history. These ideas of language draw heavily on a Foucauldian notion of discourse, explored in *The Archaeology of Knowledge*,[71] which examines ideas of knowledge, meaning, and language. The concepts in this book are applied in his later explorations of the rise of the prison, the clinic, and other social institutions.[72] I will apologize here for this extraordinarily simplistic description of Foucault's work. For the purposes of this book, however, it is the very basic idea that language, or discourse, is not a reflection of the truth, but rather formative of truth that is important.

The second concept in Bhabha's work that is central is his understanding of culture as performative. This means that he views culture as an ongoing production, rather than a fixed historical or social set of values. This approach to language and culture suggests a far different way of looking at power. Instead of viewing power as a fixed and static relationship between dominator/dominated, power is constantly being exerted by individuals and social groups. A postcolonial account of power can, therefore, take into consideration the effects of the intervention of "marginalized" peoples in the dominant discourse. If "discourse is language that had made history"[73] then one may be able to account for the transformation of Canadian Aboriginal rights discourse in the past few decades.

The link between language, culture, and power is where the intellectual contribution of Edward Said appears. In *Orientalism,* Said examines how Western narratives and accounts created Western perceptions of the Orient. He argues that these misconceptions laid the foundations for Western colonization. The idea that the control of representations has an intimate relationship with Western colonization should be familiar to those who are acquainted with Aboriginal history. The idea that the representation of Aboriginal peoples in the New World as primitive societies closer to animals than humans should certainly be recognizable. It is through these representations that the cultural extinction of Aboriginal people was authorized, by means of the theft of their land and other resources. A common critique of Said's work, however, is that he leaves no room for the colonized to represent themselves. Bhabha seeks to address this unidirectional flow of power through acknowledging the potential for marginalized peoples to represent themselves. As Young observes,

> Colonial discourse never just consisted of a set of ideological (mis)representations; its enunciations always operated as historical acts, generating specific material effects within the coercive machine of colonial rule, its enunciations, sites and formations of power simultaneously inciting material and psychological effects upon colonized subjects.[74]

The active participation of Aboriginal people in the law, politics, academics, and other cultural forms such as APTN disrupts colonial authority. It is making a new history.

Language as History

Colonialism can be described as the process of European settlement and political control over the rest of the world, including the Americas, Australia, and parts of Africa and Asia. Implicit in the process of settlement and control was the imposition of European value systems on Indigenous populations. This process required the imposition of European languages, European law, and European cultural norms. It is not necessary here to inventory the damaging policies and negative consequences that resulted. I believe, however, that it is necessary to ask the question of how resistance to this ongoing attempt at cultural genocide is possible.

A colonial regime gains its authority from the acceptance of its social and cultural values. While this may seem like an elementary insight, these social and cultural values are conveyed through language — through "discourse," to use the theoretical term. In cultural studies, theorists like Edward Said have argued that, during colonialism, European discourse had the effect of justifying the colonial dominion of Europeans through misrepresenting and subjectifying colonized peoples. Critics of this concept of colonial discourse take issue with its univocal nature. It is argued that Said's notion does not allow for an avenue whereby the misrepresented "other" can participate in their representation and thus disturb the hegemonic structures of power that are operating.

In *The Location of Culture,* however, Homi Bhabha explains how resistance to this colonial misrepresentation is not only possible, but ubiquitous and inevitable. Indeed, the core of Bhabha's critique, founded on Michel Foucault's conception of discourse, is the following:

The productivity of Foucault's concept of power/knowledge lies in its refusal of an epistemology which opposes essence/appearance, ideology/science. "Pouvoir/Savoir" places the subjects in a relation of power and recognition that is not part of a symmetrical or dialectical relation — self/other, master/slave — which can then be subverted by being inverted. Subjects are always disproportionately placed in opposition or dominations through symbolic decentering of multiple power relations which play the role of support as well as target or adversary. It becomes difficult, then, to conceive of the historical enunciations of colonial discourse without them being either functionally overdetermined or strategically elaborated or displaced by the unconscious scene of latent Orientalism. Equally, it is difficult to conceive of the process of subjectification as a placing within Orientalist or colonial discourse for the dominated subject without the dominant being strategically placed within it too. The terms in which Said's Orientalism is unified — the intentionality and unidirectionality of colonial power — also unify the subject of colonial enunciation.[75]

What Bhabha is arguing here is that the power of discourse is not a one-way street. Even though, through colonialism, European powers imposed a discourse of domination, the European invaders were not immune to the influence of Indigenous populations. Simplifying the relationship between colonizer and colonized into one homogenous discourse, eclipsing the other is not then an appropriate characterization.

Bhabha proposes that one way colonized people exert power is through what can be described as colonial splitting. This is the process whereby colonial authority is unsettled by the inappropriate application of concepts to a foreign surrounding. In law, for example, a judicial statement about land title has legal force owing to its reference to the validity of a structure of legal or sovereign power. To use a pop culture reference, in the movie *Planet 51*, Captain Chuck Baker's planting a flag on the alien planet has no meaning within the alien culture. It is a meaningless and absurd gesture because there is no cultural or legal structure to provide the action with meaning. This process can be described as

> a strategic displacement of value through a process of the metonymy of presence. It is through this partial process, represented in its enigmatic, inappropriate signifiers . . . that we begin to get a sense of a specific space of cultural colonial discourse. It is a "separate" space, a space of separation — less than one and double — which has been systematically denied by both colonists and nationalists who have sought authority in the authenticity of "origins." It is precisely as a separation from origins and essences that this colonial space is constructed.[76]

In this articulation of colonial splitting, once you separate a meaning (a truth) from its origins, the power of the authority is destabilized. To use another term coined by Bhabha, the "rules of recognition" that provide a statement with its meaning and authority are lost.

Culture as Performative

Postcolonial theorists also propose a different way to perceive "culture." Rather than perceiving culture through a list of social and behavioural characteristics that define a society, they perceive culture as a process of recreating and re-enacting some cultural practices while adapting to new situations. In the case of inter-cultural relations, this means a negotiation with other cultures.

In *The Location of Culture,* Bhabha explains,

> The social articulation of difference, from a minority perspective, is a complex, on-going negotiation that seeks to authorize cultural hybridities that emerge at moments of historical transformation. The "right" to signify from the periphery of authorized power and privilege does not depend on the persistence of tradition; it is resourced by the power of tradition to be reinscribed through the conditions of contingency and contradictoriness that attend upon the lives of those who are "in the minority." In restaging the past it introduces other incommensurable cultural temporalities into the invention of tradition. This process estranges any immediate access to an originary identity or "received" tradition. The borderline engagements of cultural difference may as often be consensual and conflictual; they may confound our definitions or tradition and modernity; realign the customary boundaries between the private and the public, high and low; and challenge normative expectations of development and progress.[77]

In other words, culture is practiced; it should "not be hastily read as the reflection of pre-given ethnic or cultural traits set on a fixed tablet of tradition."[78]

It was noted earlier that the recognition of Aboriginal rights in section 35 has been limited by a conception of "fixed" rights, from the time of European contact. While this recognition of Aboriginal rights accords with Kymlicka's normative argument for the recognition of cultural difference based on the manner of historical incorporation, this model allows for only an historical caricature of Indigenous peoples. In the *Van der Peet* case, for example, the Sto:lo were denied the right to commercial fishing — an important means by which this First Nation could be self-sufficient. In the *Pamajewon* case, the Shawanaga First Nation was denied the right of self-government, in that they could not develop gambling as a means of income revenue. Similarly, in the same case, the Eagle Lake First Nation was denied the right to economic regulation, in order to undertake similar activities.

Underlying the judgements in these decisions is the limitation of Aboriginal rights to activities that were "an integral part of the distinctive . . . society which existed prior to contact."[79] While the court does not use the term "culture," one can easily substitute this word for the phrase "distinctive society." These decisions, as was argued earlier in the chapter, take the extremely narrow view that these practices should be construed. This narrow interpretation of Aboriginal rights is deemed necessary for the "reconciliation of the pre-existence of distinctive Aboriginal societies with the assertion of Crown sovereignty."[80] The court's interpretation of this passage seems, however, to be slightly different — it seems that it is attempting to reconcile the pre-existing historical distinctive Aboriginal societies with the contemporary assertion of Crown sovereignty. Clearly, this is not reconciliation at all, but a recipe for the extinction of all contemporary Aboriginal distinctive societies.

This judicial interpretation is informed, as Bhabha says, by "terms of cultural engagement . . . read as the reflection of pre-given ethnic or cultural traits set in the fixed tablet of tradition."[81] The alternative is to understand "distinctive societies" or distinctive cultures through the eyes of cultural performativity. Culture needs to be understood as an ongoing project of reinscribing cultural values in a changing world. These traditions may be sourced in an originary identity, but ultimately they cannot be seen as a mere reflection of it. Culture, in a postcolonial understanding, can be seen as a tension between the past and present, between ontology and enunciation. As Bhabha explains,

> it is the very authority of culture as a knowledge of referential truth which is at issue in the concept and moment of enunciation. The enunciative process introduces a split in the performative present of cultural identification; a split between the traditional culturalist demand for a model, a tradition, a community, a stable system of reference, and the necessary negation of the certitude in the articulation of new cultural demands, meanings, strategies in the political present, as a practice of domination, or resistance.[82]

Culture is not a collaboration of traditional foods and fancy dress. It is a living, evolving practice of a group of people who identify as a particular cultural group. It is a constant struggle to preserve the practices that form a bond to the past, while adapting practices to meet contemporary needs. The struggle is therefore not the preservation of culture in airtight mason jars; the struggle is to support a vibrant and evolving cultural practice.

Power

I have identified two concepts that are key to understanding postcolonialism. First, language is an active force in the world, even if it is only emanating from a minority group. Second, culture should not be approached as a fixed set of traditions, but an evolving practice shared by a social group. If we accept a postcolonial concept of discourse and culture, certain assumptions about law and society need to be reconsidered. First, if we accept a postcolonial notion of discourse, everyone exercises power and influence. This not only allows for, but assumes that colonization is not just a process of iteration. Colonization creates an entirely new, hybrid society influenced by the cultures indigenous to the country. Both Indigenous and settler culture have to be seen as fluid.

It is the recognition of this fluidity that allows for a different understanding of power. With this notion of power, we see that within discourse there are always multiple points of resistance that affect the direction of society. As Foucault writes:

[w]here there is power, there is resistance, and yet, or rather consequently, this resistance is never in a position of exteriority in relation to power. Should it be said that one is always "inside" power, there is no "escaping" it, there is no absolute outside where it is concerned, because one is subject to the law in any case? Or that, history being the ruse of reason, power is the ruse of history, always emerging the winner? This would be to misunderstand the strictly relational character of power relationships. Their existence depends on a multiplicity of points of resistance: these play the role of adversary, target, support, or handle in power relations. These points of resistance are present everywhere in the power network. Hence there is no single locus of great refusal, no soul of revolt, source of all rebellions, or pure law of the revolutionary. Instead there is a plurality of resistances, each of them a special case: resistances that are possible, necessary, improbable; others that are spontaneous, savage, solitary, concerted, rampant, or violent; still others that are quick to compromise, interested, or sacrificial; by definition, they can only exist in the strategic field of power relations.[83]

So, while there is no escaping power, power is not only always the dominant party line; it is accessible to be practiced by everyone.

In relation to the analysis of Aboriginal land claims and self-government treaties, or colonized peoples in general, the insight gained from this conception of power is that within discourse we should not limit ourselves to the constricting dialectic of colonizer/colonized, but instead look at "the sphere of force relations . . . to analyze the mechanisms of power."[84] The interesting implication for the analysis of the Nisga'a Final Agreement is that we can step back from the assumption that the treaty was merely another unilateral act of force on behalf of the colonial state, and instead examine the networks of power relations that culminated in the treaty and its ongoing implementation.

Conclusion

If we accept that "truth" is produced through the interaction of language and culture, we may not be in such a fixed, legal discursive universe. In Canadian legal and political history, there has been a fairly revolutionary shift in relation to Aboriginal peoples. Assimilation has moved toward accommodation; prohibition has moved toward acceptance. While Aboriginal rights proponents quite rightly point out that this shift has its limitations in relation to the liberation of Aboriginal peoples from the chains of the colonial past, it should be recognized that there have been substantial transformations in Canadian law and society in relation to the liberation of Aboriginal peoples and Nations from the notions of colonial superiority that have affected them so negatively.

At the time of European settlement of British Columbia, the notion that Aboriginal nations had government, or had "ownership" of the land, was unthinkable. In Canadian law, it is now uniformly, though anxiously, accepted. With these transformations in mind, it needs to be recognized that marginalized peoples can affect the greater values and "truths" that the law enforces. It may be that the law is more responsive than is sometimes argued.

It will be argued in the chapters that follow that the NFA represents the creation of something new, or hybrid, to use Bhabha's term. Canadian law and society has undergone a transition to a different idea of sovereignty, which can include First Nations rather than subordinating them. This presents a challenge to try to understand what this means for the future of the Canadian nation in its new era of postcolonial sovereignty.

◇

CHAPTER TWO

Land

Introduction

It is accepted that there is a fundamental difference between Aboriginal title and Western landholding. As Dale Turner has explained, there is an essential incongruity between a liberal paradigm of ownership and Aboriginal self-government:

> Herein lies the fundamental disagreement between Aboriginal nationalists and Canadian sovereigntists: many Aboriginal peoples believe to this day that they own their lands, yet the Canadian state continues to assert and enforce its unilateral claims to sovereignty over Aboriginal lands. Interpretations of section 35(1)[1] have produced a "theory" of Aboriginal rights in Canada but have failed to reconcile these two seemingly incommensurable positions.[2]

Turner suggests that the primary ground of contest is over recognition of a concept of Aboriginal ownership that reflects a "nation to nation" relationship that recognizes the independent legitimacy of Aboriginal legal and political institutions. This "ownership" is therefore not limited to a Western understanding of ownership (a fee simple), but rather an ownership more akin to Crown or radical title. This notion of ownership therefore also imports the notion of jurisdiction.

A fee simple, as these lands are described, may be the largest estate known in law to individuals in Canada, but it is technically not the largest estate known in the law. A fee simple is limited by the powers the state exerts over the land, as they in fact are the ultimate owners of the land. The Crown holds radical or allodial title. As such, a fee simple owner's interest is affected by taxes, expropriation, police powers, and escheat.

In this chapter, the Nisga'a Final Agreement's[3] core provisions on land will be analyzed in the context of this claim. This analysis aims to examine how Nisga'a ownership is implemented in the NFA, and questions whether there is the development of a hybrid concept of land ownership that exceeds a "Western" notion of ownership by incorporating Nisga'a understandings. I argue that the land provisions in the treaty, while expressed in terms of "Western" legal ownership, also recognize a perpetual Nisga'a authority and jurisdiction over the land that is closer to a notion of Crown or radical title.

This chapter will begin with a survey of the historical context of the Nisga'a Final Agreement with the purpose of highlighting the particular social and legal background of the NFA. This section will demonstrate how there has been a sustained resistance to the assertions of Crown ownership of Nisga'a land, despite the attempts of the Canadian state to assert its sovereignty over the respective territory. This chapter will then analyze the core land provisions in the treaty. Through an analysis of these provisions, I argue that the treaty has evoked a deep ambivalence in that it is demonstrative of a hybridization of what can be called "Western" legal structures by negotiating between territorial powers and ownership rights.

Land and Sovereignty in the Nass: The Historical Context

The European settlement of the territory that was to become Canada happened over a period of around four hundred years. During this encroachment, contact with the Indigenous peoples was unavoidable. The policies applied by each group of Europeans varied, and the Indigenous peoples' response to these policies differed. As a result, to this day, there is a great variety of Indigenous peoples' statuses and rights across Canada. With such different experiences, it is important to provide a brief historical survey of the Nisga'a and their experience with European encroachment in order to reflect the particular experience of this one Aboriginal nation. This section will therefore provide a historical background that informs the negotiation and ongoing implementation of the NFA.

The Nisga'a First Nation are located in an isolated corner of British Columbia's northwest. Their traditional territory lies along the northwest coast, adjacent to Alaskan waters, and covers approximately 26,000 square kilometres. This territory, and the rights and powers maintained by the Nisga'a over this territory in the face of European encroachment, have been the subject of over 200 years of contention, when the asserting of European sovereignty and settlement began in earnest.

Similarly to other First Nations in Canada, the Nisga'a experience with Europeans began with brief interludes of primarily an economic nature. While on the Eastern front of what now comprises Canadian territory these forays had blossomed into wholesale settlement and Western political consolidation, the north-west coast of the North American continent was still in the preliminary stages of European exploration. To illustrate, it was eleven days after the Parliament of Upper Canada passed an *Act Against Slavery*[4] on July 9, 1793, thus confirming Canada as a destination for African slaves fleeing their American masters, that George Vancouver and his crew found themselves, as the result of a storm, in the Hecate Strait near the modern city of Prince Rupert. Crew members of the *Butterworth*, a trading vessel captained by a Mr. Brown, led them safely to shore. Mr. Brown, a merchant trader, who in the opinion of Vancouver employed very poor commercial practices, informed him of the residents whom he had recently encountered in the area.[5] In the course of this encounter, the alleged "improper conduct" of members of the village had led to an armed engagement "which was attended by some slaughter."[6]

The initial reports provided by Mr. Brown precipitated Vancouver's exploration of Observatory Inlet and Portland Canal that spurned some of the first European reports of the Nisga'a peoples. Vancouver, still motivated by attempts to find the north-west passage, reportedly rowed for a month before determining this goal was not to be achieved.[7] In the course of this exploration, Vancouver encountered the Nisga'a. An elaborate social engagement ensued whereby Vancouver and his crew attempted to engage in trade, and the Nisga'a attempted to determine what these new creatures that appeared at the mouth of their river actually were. As James Gosnell, past Chief and President of the then Nisga'a Tribal Council, explained, "they did not know if these people were human beings or not. Because they were different people, different type of people. Don't forget that our people had not seen the white man on earth prior to that time. They did their own quick research on the spot to see it they were human beings, and they discovered that they were human beings."[8] Vancouver's difficult trading experience marked by refusal and "disapprobation"[9] is thus explained by Raunet in the following terms:

It had been a long way to sail for a ranking officer in the Royal Navy — and one, let us not forget, who "discovered" that Vancouver Island is an island — only to be treated as a common huckster. The sovereign Nishga saw no other use for him; they had divined him human, but did not know what he thought he was for. By the time they found out, the trap was sprung.[10]

Trade ultimately motivated all of the initial forays along the northwest coast of North America.[11] The Russians, Spanish, English, and Americans began incursions, primarily interested in furs.[12] This motivation began to evolve as the race for territory became more fervent, however. When the engagements were primarily economic in nature, it did not make commercial sense to interfere with Nisga'a sovereignty over the territory. This type of behaviour only created unprofitable hostilities. As the amount of contact increased as permanent forts were established, however, territorial ambition began to become a more important priority. With increased contact with Europeans, the effects on the Aboriginal population of the area began to cause problems. The Tsimshian, neighbours of the Nisga'a who had fairly close relations with Fort Simpson, began experiencing the problems routinely associated with the introduction of Europeans and their goods — alcoholism, disease, and rampant inflation. Finally, in 1857, James Douglas, the chief factor of the Hudson's Bay Company and governor of Vancouver Island, agreed to appoint the first missionary to the area in response to these problems. Appointing this first missionary, William Duncan, opened the door for the religio-cultural aspects of European contact to begin with fervour.

In 1858, the mainland territory of British Columbia was granted colonial status as the hordes of prospectors were panning for gold along the Fraser River. James Douglas became the first Governor of the now geographically larger British Columbia, and set out to manage the situation with the Native populations. Initially, he set out to follow the policy of treaty and surrender that had begun in the early 1850s with fourteen treaties on Vancouver Island, known as the Douglas Treaties. This was the policy instituted as a result of the *Royal Proclamation* of 1763[13] whereby Indians were not to be "molested or disturbed" on their territory until it was "ceded to or purchased by" the Crown. The political and strategic motivation that existed in eastern Canada during 1763, characterized by the American threat to territory, was no longer a significant factor.[14] White settlement was frantic and the British government could afford to be thrifty. The allegiance of the peoples of the northwest coast was not a political necessity against some other Western power.

After being refused money to enter into treaty negotiations,[15] Douglas resorted to sheltering the Native populations from white encroachment through creating reserve lands. This policy continued, though with purportedly less honourable underlying intentions, on the appointment of Douglas's successor, Joseph Trutch. Trutch, fully sympathetic with colonial interests, undertook to handle the issue of the Natives. He instituted policies such as the abysmally small allotment of ten acres of land per family for the reserves, the unconsented surveying of the Native land for reserve creation, and eventually the creation of such reserves without consultation.

When it came to justifying this overt and intentional break with traditional Dominion government policy of treaty and surrender, the general trend was an uneasy pragmatism. Clement Cornwall, a Commissioner representing the Dominion of Canada for the Royal Commission of the Inquiry into the North-West Coast Indians, created in 1887, wrote,

> But to return to the question of the Indian title to lands. It has been determined that Government cannot in any way allow this. There is no ground for the assertion that the fee in the lands ever rested in the natives although in many parts of the old Provinces of Canada the Indian title was, as it is called, extinguished by the force of purchasing the same for infinitesimally small sums, and a like course has been pursued in the North West Territories, yet it has not by any means been done all over those provinces, and where it has been done it was only, I conceive, because it was deemed politic and expedient to do so. No doubt it would have been politic and expedient to do so in this Province years ago, but it was not done, and now, one would say, it is impossible to do it. The mere idea of the necessity of such a course invalidates at once every title and real property in the country, although those titles have been granted by the Crown. Which is absurd.
>
> The Indian in his wild state has no idea of property in or title to land. . . . The beasts of the field have as much ownership in the land as he has. [16]

Here we see some of pragmatic reasons for the portrayal of the Indian as a wild, untamable savage — the need to protect Crown-based title to land. The discourse that supports this assertion is one that characterizes Aboriginal peoples as mere wild beasts rather than human beings living in organized societies. First Nations did not, therefore, just have to establish their claim to land and self-government, but to basic humanity.

The European version of Aboriginal peoples' relationship to the land varied drastically from the Aboriginal one. In traditional Nisga'a *Ayuukhlw* (law and custom), there is an intimate tie between the land and political and legal organization. The Nisga'a had an elaborate social organization founded on the relationship to the land.

In Nisga'a society, there are several levels of social organization. The largest is the Nisga'a Nation. The Nisga'a Nation is then composed of four villages, which are New Aiyansh, Gitwinsilkh, Laxalzap, and Gingolx. There are four pdeek (clans or tribes) — Ganada (Raven/Frog), Laxgibuu (Wolf/Bear), Gisk'aast (Killer Whale/Owl), and Laxsgiik (Eagle/Beaver). There are also wilps (houses), which are Nisga'a matrilineal family groups. There were also traditionally wilnaat'ahl, which were other groupings of houses that were offshoots or amalgams of other wilps. Finally, there is the nuclear family. An individual's membership in these groups, and one's rank in these groups, determines both access to resources and political position. These social groupings organized the political and economic fabric of Nisga'a culture, which in Nisga'a society were interminably intertwined.[17]

The chiefs of the clans, for example, traditionally held responsibility for the areas of land controlled by the clan. The chief oversaw the apportionment of rights and access to the land as mandated by Nisga'a Ayuukhlw. The role of chief, however, should not be seen as one of ownership or power over the land. Indeed, the role of chief is one of great responsibility. As Sharon McIvor, the leader of the Native Women's Association of Canada, is reported as saying,

> "I have . . . come to the conclusion that the terms we're speaking of are non-aboriginal terms," McIvor argues. This is particularly true about concepts of power, she contends. "Power" is not a concept that reflects the culture or traditions of aboriginal people. The idea of responsibility for "the way we live" is a much more appropriate one, McIvor maintains, and it points to the only real way that aboriginal peoples can obtain greater control over their lives — by taking responsibility for their own communities and the pressing issues in their everyday lives.[18]

The role of chief in Nisga'a Ayuukhlw involves a great deal of responsibility for the well being of the group. A Nisga'a who was in line for a chieftainship was expected to be very successful, as this was an indication that they would ensure the prosperity of the clan. One of the primary responsibilities of a chief, for example, was the allocation and management of resources:

In the old days, when the wilp or house families all lived together and represented the basic Nisga'a economic unit, people were aware of what harvesting activities were currently going on and what areas had been harvested in past years. The social structure provided the chief and his sub-chiefs with an access to information about the conditions of various animal populations on different areas of the ango'oskw. In short, they had access to the types of information that was required to manage the ango'oskw animal and plant resources.

It was part of the chief's responsibilities to control the harvest on the ango'oskw. He organized the hunting and trapping parties and decided which areas will be harvested, and when the timing was right to harvest particular seasonal resources.[19]

The notion of "ownership of land" was thus intimately tied with political power and responsibility. The land was not simply owned by an individual or family, but was managed and controlled by larger political units for the betterment of the clan or house.

Regardless of Aboriginal government, the slow encroachment on Nisga'a land and resources continued. Reciprocally, the Nisga'a protest against such encroachment became more sophisticated. From the beginning of white attempts to partition, grant, sell, allocate, and license rights to Nisga'a resources and territory, the Nisga'a insisted that these actions were contrary to the true ownership of the land. Actions taken by the Nisga'a included petitions, participation in Royal Commissions, and even hiring the London Law firm of Fox and Preece to present a petition of behalf of the Nisga'a to the Privy Council. This petition, dated January 22nd, 1913, stated that "[f]rom time immemorial the said Nation or Tribe of Indians exclusively possessed, occupied and used and exercised sovereignty over that portion of the territory now forming the Province of British Columbia which is included in the following limits,"[20] and then proceeded to describe their territory. This petition was made directly to the Privy Council. From a Nisga'a perspective, the sovereign responsible for the incursions on their land should be the authority to deal with it. Further, they were of the view that a remote court may have been less influenced by the local settlers.[21] From the initiation of white encroachment, the message of the Nisga'a was the same: "Saayeen! Saayeen!"[22]

The Nisga'a position on the ownership of their land has been unwavering since early contact with Europeans. In Nisga'a history, it is recorded that K'amganxminmuxw once said that "[t]he Government has nothing to do with our land."[23] This statement made by K'amganxminmuxw reflects the very central Nisga'a belief in relation to Nisga'a lands. Indeed, years of protest, struggle, litigation, legal enactments, and political maneuvering have been undertaken on behalf of this one crucial statement. This contention can be illustrated by a linguistic difference between Nisga'a and Canadian terminology. In Euro-Canadian legal terminology, the phrase "land claim" is the common parlance to describe Indigenous struggles with the Canadian government over land. The Nisga'a, however, have always insisted that their dispute with the government of Canada is not a "land claim," but rather "the land question." This is because to claim something implies that entitlement to that thing has been lost. The Nisga'a, however, have never lost their land, and only desired to settle the question of the land with the Canadian and provincial governments that in fairly recent history have claimed sovereignty over it.[24] Indeed, as early as 1913, the Nisga'a were petitioning the Privy Council to recognize their "tribal ownership" of "all fisheries and other natural resources" in the "Valley of the Nass River" in order to "open the way for [the Nisga'a to take] our place not only as loyal British subjects but also Canadian citizens as for many years [they] desired to do."[25] The responses to this claim, however, were far from favourable, as the Nisga'a conception of title exceeded the limitations of any Aboriginal right the government was willing to recognize. Duncan C. Scott, Deputy Superintendent General, responded to this claim:

From these words it will become apparent what fancies occupy the minds of the Indians when they think of the aboriginal title and its purchase.

The Privy Council, to which the Nishga Nation desire to appeal, has already pronounced upon the nature of the Indian title, describing it as a "personal and usufructary right dependent of the goodwill of the sovereign."

It follows that the Indian title, when acknowledged by the Crown, cannot be separated from what the Crown elects to grant. In appraising Indian title we should go back to the time when the lands were a wilderness, when we find a wild people upon an unimproved estate. The Indian title cannot increase in value with civilized development; cession of Indian territory has always preceded the settlement of the country and whatever has been granted for the transfer has represented the good will of the Crown, not the intrinsic value of the land at the time of the cession, and assuredly not the value enhanced by the activities of the white population. From the earliest times the beneficial interest has ever been appraised by the Crown, the Indians accepting what was offered, with upon occasion, slight alteration in terms previously fixed by the Crown. It is optional, when, if at all, the Crown may proceed to extinguish Indian title, and, therefore, if it is decided that the Indians of British Columbia have a title of this nature there can be no claim for deferred benefit from the Crown.[26]

In this statement we can clearly see the position of the Department of Indian Affairs on the rights of the Nisga'a to their land in the early twentieth century. The Nisga'a were entirely at the mercy of the good will of the Crown, which recognized no inherent rights to the land they had traditionally occupied.

Despite, and possibly as a result of, Nisga'a resistance, the first half of the twentieth century saw the bleakest time for the Nisga'a land question. With the publication of the 1915 Nisga'a petition to the Privy Council, both the federal and provincial governments closed ranks. The *St. Catherine's Milling*[27] case had pronounced in 1888 that Aboriginal title was merely a "personal and usufructary right dependent on the goodwill of the Sovereign,"[28] and was trotted out in a wholesale denial of Nisga'a rights. Native agitation continued until a modification to the *Indian Act*[29] was used to forcibly put the issue to rest. This came in the form of the 1927 addition of section 141 of the *Indian Act*. This section made illegal the procuring or collecting of money for the purpose of Indian land claims. In the same year, draconian legislation was also passed banning any form of Indian festival, which would have prohibited even the funeral customs of the Nisga'a.[30] Any form of legal protest was quashed, while the law also assisted in the attempt to culturally cripple the vivacity that the Nisga'a had theretofore demonstrated.

In the Nass Valley, however, it would be erroneous to assume that the law was a major hindrance to the continuation of Nisga'a traditions. The legal prohibition of culturally important festivals such as feasting did not stop Nisga'a celebrations. Deanna Nyce, the Chief Executive Officer of the Wilp Wilxo'oskwhl Nisga'a, reported that despite these legal prohibitions feasts and celebrations were still held. Chief James Gosnell stated in 1981,

There were many people, not necessarily Nishga people, but Indian people throughout B.C. were imprisoned because of the practice of our own culture, the potlatch, as they call it in other parts. But it is not all of it, it's only part of it. . . . Our people never did abide by those, they call them Potlatch Laws. You know, our people carried out their tradition all the time. That's how we were able to maintain some of it, or most of it until right now. They never did abide by those laws. In those days, they had these so-called "Indian agents" going in there and telling people that it is unlawful, so people just ignored it. And now during that period of time, and until 1958, we were totally isolated, there's no road, or anyway, the only transportation was the river. We were totally isolated. So on the basis of isolation, we were able to just carry on our traditions, our way of life in respect to potlatch and that sort of things.[31]

Therefore, while legal prohibitions on Indian festivals were an important aspect of the Canadian government's attempts to control and assimilate Aboriginal peoples, it is important to recognize that these attempts were not very successful.

With the revision of the *Indian Act* in 1951, the Nisga'a again gained the legal capacity to pursue land claims when section 141 was repealed. The interim period had, however, created new obstacles. The repeal of this section allowed the Nisga'a to once again collect money to pursue a legal resolution to the land question. The legal deliberation of the claim, however, came with risks. If the court decided that the *St. Catherine's Milling* case was to be followed, not only the Nisga'a would have to live with the crippling result, all Aboriginal rights in Canada would be affected. The chance of losing in the courts led to the loss of the support of the Native Brotherhood, who refused to assent to an action that could lead to such potentially damaging consequences.[32] Despite losing the support of other Aboriginal organizations, the Nisga'a persisted.

With the governments, both provincial and federal, holding to their stance that the unilateral assertion that Crown sovereignty eclipsed any rights the Nisga'a had over the territory, legal action was determined necessary. While through the course of the century, as the one before, at politically convenient intervals small inducements to placate the Natives were offered, they always came with a fairly high price. To refer the Nisga'a petition formally to the Privy Council, as was procedurally necessary, for example, the government tried to extract a promise that the Nisga'a would surrender their title even if it was found that they indeed had ownership of it. These small incentives also fundamentally failed to address the heart of the land question that had been consistently reiterated since early contact with Europeans — the unbending view of the Nisga'a that the land was, as it had always been, theirs. In the face of government refusal to address the issue, the 1951 changes to the *Indian Act* once again allowed the Nisga'a to pursue a legal resolution.

The litigation that ensued was to become one of the landmark cases for Aboriginal land rights in Canada. Frank Calder, a man steeped from an early age in the Nisga'a land question, brought a case asking the court to issue "a declaration that the aboriginal title (also known as Indian title) of the Plaintiffs to their ancient tribal territory has never been lawfully extinguished."[33] This, he further claimed, would entitle them to the full traditional rights to the lands, as they were never surrendered through treaty or any other manner. Despite the earlier precedent in the *St. Catherine's Milling Case*, the Supreme Court delivered an ambiguous judgement. The Nisga'a argued that Aboriginal title flowed from occupation from time immemorial. This interest was protected by the *Royal Proclamation* of 1763[34] from alienation except by surrender to the Crown. As the land had not been surrendered or extinguished in any manner, Nisga'a title had never been extinguished. Justices Judson, Martland, and Ritchie held that the *Royal Proclamation* did not extend to the territories that were not part of British territory as of 1763. Since the colonial status of British Columbia was not determined until the nineteenth century, the Justices reasoned, the *Royal Proclamation* did not apply. In addition, they determined that any Aboriginal interest had henceforth been extinguished by sovereign exercise of power inconsistent with Aboriginal rights. Justices Hall, Spence, and Laskin, in contrast, determined that the *Royal Proclamation* did indeed apply, and was not thenceforth extinguished by surrender or specific legislation. The court was split equally on the characterization and status of Aboriginal interests. The case was ultimately decided on a different legal point. Justice Pigeon wrote a procedural decision that the court had no jurisdiction to grant a declaration contrary to Crown title without a fiat from the Lieutenant Governor of the Province in accordance with the *Crown Proceedings Act, 1960*. Justices Judson, Martland, and Ritchie did not concur with him, but because of their judgement and Pigeon's, the Nisga'a claim failed.

The legal proceedings were only a part of the history of this turbulent period in Native-Canadian relations. Between the time the case was initiated in 1967 and judgement handed down in 1973, matters of Aboriginal status within the Canadian state were coming to a head. Native political and legal agitation had led to several government initiatives on Native entitlements, culminating in the infamous White Paper of June 1969. In this, the federal government outlined its initiative to abolish "Indian" as a legally significant category, thus, in the opinion of the government, eliminating the discrimination and "special treatment" that "has made of the Indians a community disadvantaged and apart."[35] Aboriginal peoples had an entirely different view of the proposals. Abolition of the *Indian Act*, in the view of most of the Aboriginal communities in Canada, would compromise their ability to maintain their distinct identities within the Canadian state. The White Paper proposals were viewed as another attempt to fully assimilate Aboriginal peoples into the Canadian "melting pot." Response to the document was swift and vituperative. Harold Cardinal, an Aboriginal activist, wrote a powerful rejoinder to this policy paper that helped to consolidate a Canada-wide stance against this move that threatened Aboriginals "special" status.[36] Aboriginal peoples, therefore, opened up a "third space" of enunciation which "displaced the narrative of the Western nation"[37] as moving toward a homogenous melting pot where "Indianness" was no longer important.

In view of the Aboriginal uprising against the proposals contained in the White Paper, and the legal and political stance on recognizing Aboriginal land title, government policy took a radical turn. On August 8, 1973, Prime Minister Trudeau announced that the government would negotiate with groups who had not signed treaties.[38] The first of these treaties to be concluded was with the James Bay Cree and the Inuit of Northern Quebec.[39] This treaty was precipitated by a successful court action resulting in the James Bay Cree being granted an injunction halting a multi-billion dollar Hydro-Quebec project. The treaty was negotiated swiftly to prevent further expensive delays.[40] This treaty provided monetary compensation for lost land, and some other allowances in social areas, but was criticized almost universally as a truly bad bargain for the James Bay Cree and the Inuit of Northern Quebec.[41]

While the federal government had adopted a policy of comprehensive land claims in 1976, the Nisga'a would not see the fruits of this policy shift for another two decades. During this time, the federal government would recognize and affirm existing Aboriginal and treaty rights in the Constitution,[42] the British Columbia government would initiate the B.C. Treaty Commission to act as an impartial body to help create a new relationship of mutual respect between First Nations and government,[43] and the courts would further refine the legal landscape of Native rights.[44]

While the legal status of Aboriginal rights and title was being deliberated in the political and legal sphere, the Nisga'a continued to negotiate with the provincial and federal governments. In 1991, the Nisga'a Framework Agreement was signed, defining the scope, subject matter, and process to be followed. Notably, this framework agreement put the issue of Nisga'a self-government onto the list of issues that were to be discussed. This led to the Nisga'a Agreement in Principle signed in 1996. This document laid out the basic relationship that was to become more fully elaborated in the NFA initialed on August 4, 1998. On May 11, 2000, the NFA finally came into effect.

While the Nisga'a would remain a part of the Canadian constitutional order, this treaty would fundamentally change the relationship between the Nisga'a and the federal and provincial governments. The Agreement in Principle and the Nisga'a Final Agreement are both clear that the Nisga'a would continue to be subject to Canadian constitutional law. This means that the Nisga'a continue to be Aboriginal peoples under section 35 of the Constitution guaranteeing Aboriginal and treaty rights. The understanding reached also mandates that Nisga'a institutions are subject to the *Canadian Charter of Rights and Freedoms*. Notably, the NFA also states that the agreement does not alter the Constitution of Canada in regard to the division of powers between the federal and provincial governments. The NFA, however, does constitute the Nisga'a Lisims Government as a legal and political institution competent to legislate, and makes the Nisga'a Lisims Government the "principal authority"[45] to legislate on Nisga'a land, language, culture, and citizenship, among other powers. Approximately 2,000 square kilometres were deemed Nisga'a lands, or lands owned by the Nisga'a Nation. The Nisga'a maintained 16,101 square kilometres of hunting land, and 26,838 square kilometres in fishing area. In addition, the entire Nass Area is a co-managed area with the province of British Columbia. As Kevin McKay, Nisga'a Lisims Government chairperson, has said, maintaining the supremacy of the Constitution of Canada does not weigh heavily upon their treaty success, as "we wanted to negotiate our way into Canada, not out of it."[46]

As this historical survey suggests, despite the attempts of the Canadian federal and provincial governments to frustrate the Nisga'a desire to settle the land question, they persevered. Nisga'a resistance to the "ideological discourses of modernity" seems rooted in Nisga'a culture and traditions, which even a hundred years of colonial bureaucracy could not extinguish.

Land Provisions in the NFA

Nisga'a resistance to the colonial bureaucratic and legal regime was sustained, even throughout the most oppressive phases of colonial assimilation. At the core of this resistance was the land question. The land provisions in the NFA are therefore of central significance in exploring the treaty.

In this section, I argue that the land provisions in the NFA mediate between a Nisga'a understanding of land "ownership" and the Western legal construct of it. I argue that the NFA represents a hybridizations of "Western" legal structures by implementing a landholding regime which negotiates between jurisdiction and ownership. In other terms, the land provisions in the NFA mediate between a construct of power and rights. It is in this negotiation that we see the creation of a deep ambivalence in Canadian legal and political discourse.

In this section, I will examine the core land provisions in the Nisga'a Final Agreement by comparing them to the ordinary deployment of such arrangements in Canadian law. This comparison will show that the Nisga'a core land provisions are a hybrid between jurisdiction and ownership, that allow for Nisga'a collective ownership within a legal framework intended to implement individual land rights.

It must be said, however, that it is difficult to get an understanding of the general effect of the treaty provisions from examining provisions individually. According to Tom Molloy, the lead negotiator for the Canadian government, this is a result of the general approach taken in the treaty. He explains that the treaty took a "Modified Aboriginal Rights Approach."[47] He describes this approach as one where "rights are agreed to rather than extinguished, rendering obsolete the troublesome phrase of 'cede, release, and surrender.' The Nisga'a have not surrendered their rights to the land they have occupied since time immemorial; rather, the right has been modified to specify a particular area over which their rights of ownership continue to prevail."[48] The result is,

> Given the nature of the certainty provisions, it might be useful to look at how they weave together to form the fabric of certainty. For those interested in object lessons — politicians take note — this will also demonstrate the importance in treaties of reviewing the entire document, for discussing or attacking one clause on its own is a meaningless exercise.[49]

A discussion of the core land provisions cannot be done without reference to other aspects of the treaty, such as Nisga'a governance, which will follow.

The largest estate in land in the treaty is Nisga'a Lands. These lands, being approximately 1,992 square kilometres, are defined as follows:

> On the effective date, the Nisga'a Nation owns Nisga'a Lands in fee simple, being the largest estate known in law. This estate is not subject

to any condition, proviso, restriction, exception, or reservation set out in the Land Act, or any comparable limitation under any federal or provincial law. No estate or interest in Nisga'a Lands can be expropriated except as permitted by, and in accordance with, this Agreement.[50]

This may not seem like a provision that would be ultimately advantageous to the Nisga'a Nation. A fee simple, in Canadian legal terms, while being the largest private landholding mechanism in the law, does not, at first glance, seem radically different than the interest many people hold in their homes. The difference, however, lies in the communal ownership of the lands, rather than the individual members of the Nation owning the land.

While describing Nisga'a land ownership may not seem to implement a very "Aboriginal" form of ownership, by comparing the core land provisions to the characteristics of Aboriginal title in the *Delgamuukw* case, we can begin to appreciate how fee simple ownership in the NFA is implementing a hybrid version of land ownership. In *Delgamuukw*, the three aspects of *sui generis* Aboriginal title are: 1) Aboriginal title is communally held; 2) Aboriginal title cannot be alienated to anyone except the Crown; and 3) the source of Aboriginal title is "the prior occupation of Canada by Aboriginal peoples."[51]

Nisga'a core lands are held in fee simple by the Nisga'a Nation. The Nisga'a Nation is the owner of the core lands. The definition of the Nisga'a Nation in the treaty is "the collectivity of those Aboriginal people who share the language, culture and laws of the Nisga'a Indians of the Nass Area, and their descendants."[52] The Nisga'a people own the land. At a basic level, this is communally held Aboriginal title. A Nisga'a fee simple is not, then, the equivalent of a normal fee simple in land. The closest comparable right would be a fee simple held by a corporation. Indeed, in Canadian law there is precedent for communal landholding being effected through corporate ownership. In the *Hofer*[53] case, for example, a Hutterite colony held their assets as a corporation. When they excommunicated a member, the Supreme Court held that an expelled member of a Hutterite colony had no claim to the assets that he brought into the colony. The logic deployed was that the member had agreed to the terms of the articles of incorporation which added his assets to the communal wealth. He could not therefore take such assets with him if he was to leave the colony. On a fundamental level, a corporation, which is an organization with directors that control assets for the benefit of a community, is indeed a form of communal land rights. Nisga'a fee simple land is not simply corporate ownership.

On a basic level, the *Hofer* case and the NFA land provisions both present a challenge to an individualistic liberal notion of land ownership. As Kymlicka writes, "It is far from clear that the Hutterite claim can be defended within the language of Rawls's 'political liberalism.'"[54] This is the frontier of rights discourse where group rights collide with individual rights. While this is an aspect of the NFA that has created debate, this tension between group rights and individual freedom is, not surprisingly, where we find the basic challenge to colonial authority.

A greater challenge to colonial authority is found in the nature of Nisga'a fee simple. Nisga'a fee simple seems to be contrary to the second characteristic, in that Aboriginal title cannot be alienated to anyone except the Crown. Some background is required, however, to understand this characteristic, as it has a historical origin.

The requirement that Indian land must be ceded to the Crown originated in early European settlement in eastern Canada. It has been argued that this policy emerged as a result of the British Crown's legal conquest of the sovereign tribes in Eastern Canada. Indeed, First Nations were sovereign prior to the victory of the English over the French in the French-Indian War (also called the Seven Years' War) in 1763. Once Britain had consolidated its power over Canadian territory, it was important to pacify the First Nations that made this victory possible. The *Royal Proclamation* of 1763 therefore guaranteed Aboriginal peoples their land, unless properly ceded to the Crown. This had the effect of subsuming First Nations under the sovereignty of the British Crown. As Borrows describes, this equated "Aboriginal sovereignty and subordination."[55] Harring writes:

> This law centred policy as it pertained to native people has two purposes: first, to avoid unnecessary colonial wars by protecting indigenous people from uncontrolled usurpation of their lands by local colonists; and second to re-socialize indigenous people so as to accommodate them to the new colonial order. Law, as an instrument of social control, took an equal place with education and religion in the acculturation of indigenous people.[56]

The surrender of Aboriginal title only to the Crown therefore both reflects First Nations sovereign status and represents the means of its subordination.

The core land provisions in the NFA, arguably, do not represent a surrender of Aboriginal title to the Crown,[57] yet they do free Nisga'a lands from the requirement of Crown cession. As Molloy explains, the NFA is a modified rights approach to Aboriginal title. The NFA sets out Nisga'a existing Aboriginal rights, rather than surrendering them. The Nisga'a title to land is therefore defined and continued, rather than being surrendered to the Crown. Paradoxically, while the Nisga'a Nation can "dispose of its estate in fee simple on any parcel of Nisga'a Lands to any person,"[58] "a parcel of Nisga'a Lands does not cease to be Nisga'a Lands as a result of any change in ownership of an estate or interest in that parcel."[59] As a result, the Nisga'a can sell a fee simple in Nisga'a Lands, but the land does not cease to be Nisga'a Land. Thus, while the land is transferable, it is never transferred from Nisga'a jurisdiction.

The only comparable type of interest in Western landholding is radical or allodial title. This is the Crown's ultimate ownership of the land. As Justice Brennan describes in *Mabo (No. 2)*,

> There is a distinction between the Crown's title to a colony and the Crown's ownership of land in the colony, as Roberts-Wray points out (74) *ibid.*, p 625:
>
> > "If a country is part of Her Majesty's dominions, the sovereignty vested in her is of two kinds. The first is the power of government. The second is title to the country. . . .
> >
> > This ownership of the country is radically different from ownership of the land: the former can belong only to a sovereign, the latter to anyone. Title to land is not, per se, relevant to the constitutional status of a country; land may have become vested in the Queen, equally in a Protectorate or in a Colony, by conveyance or under statute."[60]

What this reiteration of domestic and international law on radical title ultimately suggests is that radical title has two aspects. The first is land as territory, the second is land as property — power over land versus ownership over land. The Nisga'a Nation ultimately are recognized to possess aspects of both in Nisga'a core lands.

For example, the NFA provides that the Nisga'a Nation have the right to escheat in all but name only. Escheat is the reversion of any land when there are no heirs or assigns upon the death of a property holder. In the Nisga'a Final Agreement, this Crown right of reversion is avoided by a provision in the treaty that states that any Nisga'a Land that escheats to the Crown will be transferred, with no charge, to the Nisga'a government.[61] This rule protects the core Nisga'a land base. Through this provision, at least in this respect, the Nisga'a Lisims Government has one very important stick in the "bundle of rights" that the Crown holds.

Thus, while at first glance it may appear that the recognition of a Nisga'a fee simple in core Nisga'a Lands does not really provide the Nisga'a Lisims Government with much more than an ordinary individual or corporation, for example, the "bundle of rights" attached to these lands are greatly expanded by other "public power" provisions in the treaty. We can observe the usage of a common Canadian legal construct — the fee simple — that on further examination no longer looks so familiar. The Nisga'a interest recognized in the treaty by the term "fee simple," under scrutiny, exceeds the limits of a typical, garden-variety fee simple. This is because the Nisga'a do not only gain a "fee simple" in terms of ownership, but also a territorial right more similar to that held by the Crown.[62]

The potential for the commercialization of Nisga'a Lands, however, has caused concern among academic commentators. Indeed, Rynard's main critique of the NFA land provisions is that Nisga'a Lands are brought into the familiar Canadian legal structures that, in his view, threaten the integrity and adequacy of Aboriginal land:

> Judging from the content of the Nisga'a treaty, it is clear that Canadian political and corporate elites do not want to have to deal with evolving concepts of Aboriginal rights to land. They continue to demand that the lands of Aboriginal peoples be brought into the familiar and predictable reach of crown sovereignty and Canadian property law. This is probably because it is on the basis of a distinct title with pre-contact origins — along with a jurisdictional component relevant over large areas — that the rights and aspirations of First Nations would pose a fundamental challenge to established socio-economic and political practices. The lack of progress at the end of the twentieth century on land rights issues is deeply troubling and demonstrates that First Nations relations have not been immune to the corporate agenda which has dominated other areas of Canadian policy making.[63]

Rynard fears that "[t]he loss of most of the traditional territories, combined with the goal of reducing Nisga'a fiscal dependence on the federal and provincial governments, will create enormous pressures to exploit the resources of

Nisga'a lands in ways which may be ecologically unsustainable given market imperatives."[64]

The potential "commercialization" of Nisga'a Land, however, plays an important role in Nisga'a self-sufficiency. One of the pragmatic problems with reserve land under the *Indian Act* was that it could not be used as collateral for investment. Indeed, under the *Indian Act*, any development of the land was regulated by the Indian and Northern Affairs bureaucracy. As Raunet explains,

> Until the postwar reform, the Indian Act specified that the Indian was "not a person." Barred from the polling station, from the banks, and from the bars, he was comparable in status to a minor. The restrictions placed a crucial role in keeping Native people at a low stage of economic development. Nishga Harry Nyce's father, for example, purchased a gillnet boat. He did not have financial help, collateral. He had to go the Department of Indian Affairs to have his qualifications documented. He had to go to the fishing company to obtain their backing, and he had to have the permission of the Superintendent of Indian Affairs in the Rupert District to borrow money or to get in any kind of financial transaction.
>
> Nowadays an Indian can borrow money by himself. But he still faces the problem of collateral. He does not have clear title to his house or his land on the reserve. Natives have tried to circumvent this difficulty, but they still face a handicap in their dealings with the banks.[65]

This lack of clear title that can be used as collateral has been identified by Hernendo de Soto as a major obstacle to the economic development of peoples in many Third World countries.[66] This situation, however, was precipitated in a "First World" country by an intentional set of paternalistic laws. Therefore, while the NFA allows for Nisga'a Lands to be alienated, it also allows for the Nisga'a to economically develop by using the value of the land as collateral.

Therefore, while group rights do not represent a fundamental challenge to colonial authority, the territorial powers attached to a Nisga'a fee simple seem to create an uneasy ambivalence. On the one hand, Nisga'a rights to the land seem to mimic Western notions of ownership too closely. So closely that there are concerns that commercialization will undermine the cultural success of the Nisga'a Nation. These provisions, on the other hand, allow for the Nisga'a Nation's viability through economic development. As Ron Nyce, Chief Councillor and hereditary chief, reflected,

> Today . . . a young Nisga'a guy can apply to buy a tow boat to take logs out to the big ships, he used to hire out. . . . We want to circulate income within the nation instead of taking it out. Outsiders look at the feasting system which circulates money in the community — up to $76,000 an evening. Each community will have it filter back to them.[67]

He even mused that he would be happy to see Nisga'a shopping malls, and buy a car in a Nisga'a car lot before he dies. Whether this type of economic development will be seen as the cultural success of the Nisga'a Nation by others is more problematic. This debate has become even more important since the Nisga'a Lisims Government has allowed for the *Nisga'a Landholding Transition Act, 2009*, which allows for Nisga'a citizens to hold their land within Nisga'a lands in fee simple.

The third characteristic of Aboriginal title in the *Delgamuukw* case is the source of title — prior occupation. It is this grounding of Nisga'a title that ultimately disturbs colonial authority. Nisga'a entitlement to Nisga'a Lands is clearly rooted in prior occupation. Nisga'a Land rights, along with all the other rights in the treaty, are a result of the recognition of continuing Nisga'a rights and powers over the territory they have held since time immemorial. The origin of the power and rights in the NFA is not colonial authority, but the recognition of the limitation of it. Indeed, it is the source of Aboriginal title that makes it so problematic. Nisga'a Land provisions look so similar, yet are so foreign and threatening. Nisga'a core lands are expressed in terms of individual liberal landholding, yet implement communal tenure. Nisga'a core lands are called "fee simple" lands, yet are overlaid with aspects of radical title. Nisga'a Lands allow for "Western" economic development, yet also potentially support Nisga'a cultural revival. It is the "disavowed knowledges [that] return to make the presence of authority uncertain."[68] Aboriginal rights and title, vociferously resisted in the early twentieth century as being "absurd," and "with no grounds for the assertion that the fee in the lands ever rested in the natives,"[69] have emerged to compete with assertions of colonial sovereignty.

Conclusion

In *The Location of Culture*, Homi Bhabha describes how assertions of English novels in India both asserted the symbols of English imperialism, yet ultimately betrayed "signs of a discontinuitous history, an estrangement of the English."[70] He describes these novels as revealing a "disturbance of [their] authoritative representations by the uncanny forces of race, sexuality, violence, cultural and even climatic difference which emerge in the colonial discourse as the mixed and split texts of hybridity."[71] The displacement of colonial authority, according to Bhabha, creates an ambivalence, or a "split between its appearance as original and authoritative and its articulation as repetition and difference."[72] The NFA's land provisions are an expression of colonial authority imbued with such an ambivalence. While the provisions reproduce Western legal strategies, and the authority with which they claim power, the provisions also simultaneously exhibit the limitations of the authority and transparency of these strategies. As Bhabha explains, mimicry

> emerges as a question of colonial authority, an agonistic space. To the extent to which discourse is a form of defensive warfare, mimicry marks these moments of civil disobedience within the discipline of civility: signs of spectacular resistance. Then the words of the master become a site of hybridity — the warlike, subaltern sign of the native — then we may not only read between the lines but even seek to change the often coercive reality that they so lucidly contain.[73]

The land provisions in the treaty are a moment of "civil disobedience." The NFA asserts the symbols of Western landholding, but yet ultimately betrays "signs of a discontinuitous history, an estrangement of the English."[74] The NFA represents the estrangement of colonial law which has been disturbed by cultural difference. The power of law is now "split between its appearance as original and authoritative and its articulation as repetition and difference."[75] The NFA's land provisions reproduce Western legal strategies, but undermine the authority with which they claim power. The NFA mimics the language of colonial power, but ultimately claims the authority away from the colonial regime by doing so. This, indeed, is the origin of a productive postcolonial ambivalence.

This ambivalence is at the core of the criticism of the NFA from the Canadian legal establishment, as well as Aboriginal rights scholars. A common criticism of the treaty is that the Nisga'a only garnered full ownership over ten per cent of Nisga'a traditional lands. In an interview with Kevin McKay, the Speaker of the Wilp Si'ayuukhl Nisga'a (the legislative arm of the Nisga'a Lisims Government), he responded to this criticism by stating that "if non-Nisga'a could have a better understanding of the premise of the land question then they could have a better acceptance of the NFA."[76] This is a history, according to him, that had always been willing to find ways to co-exist with newcomers. As he explained, "now that there are white people here, there is a question about the land."[77] In relation to the NFA, he stated that it is a "political accord between three parties, it was necessary to compromise," and "the negotiators made the agreement innovative" in order to reflect Nisga'a goals.

A better answer to this criticism of the treaty lies in the nature of Nisga'a land. As was argued in the previous section, Nisga'a lands may be expressed in Western terms of ownership, yet they are overlaid with the powers of government. The land question was about "negotiating [the Nisga'a Nation's] way into Canada." Land rights, according to Kevin McKay, are not simply expressed as ownership rights in the Western model, but as political power. The "right" to the land, with its origin in the pre-existing "sovereignty" of the Nisga'a people, is a springboard that the Nisga'a used to gain political recognition within the Canadian federation. If we refer back to Rynard's critiques that the treaty does not sufficiently reflect Aboriginal difference, and merely subsumes Nisga'a rights into the Canadian legal and political order, this, it would seem, was not the unfortunate result, but rather an explicit goal. The treaty is a doorway to political recognition, not simply the definition of rights to land. While no one can foresee the effects of this treaty, in the opinion of Kevin McKay, the treaty is "not a book of guarantees, but a book of opportunities."[78] Even Rynard, with his critique of the treaty, voices the opinion that "[g]iven a political climate hostile to Aboriginal rights, the treaty is a significant achievement and deserves the support of fair-minded Canadians."[79]

○

CHAPTER THREE

Rights

Introduction

Aboriginal rights other than land have been recognized in Canadian jurisprudence through a historic notion of Aboriginal culture. In chapter one, this was described as the "frozen rights" approach, where Aboriginal rights are recognized based on the essential cultural practices of these groups prior to European contact. Canadian law is therefore protecting the culture of First Nations that existed hundreds of years ago, but failing to enable the possibility of modern First Nation survival. This approach reflects an understanding of the concept of a culture as static rather than performative and dynamic. This chapter will trace how the Nisga'a Final Agreement has evaded a static characterization of First Nation culture through balancing the protection of historical culture with the creation of a sustainable contemporary economy.

In the previous chapter it was argued that the NFA's core land provisions are a hybrid of Western and Nisga'a conceptions of land and landholding. Nisga'a core lands, however, are just one type of right contained in the treaty. Nisga'a core lands, as discussed in the previous chapter, are the lands that the Nisga'a have both territorial and ownership rights over. These 2,000 square kilometres, are only ten per cent of the 20,000 square kilometres of the Nisga'a Nation's traditional lands. Over the remaining 18,000 square kilometres the Nisga'a Nation has various Aboriginal rights. For example, there is approximately 16,000 square kilometres of Nass Wildlife Area where the Nisga'a has co-management and hunting rights. The Nisga'a also have fishing rights over approximately 26,000 square kilometres. This chapter will examine Nisga'a rights to resources both within Nisga'a core lands and in these remaining co-management areas.

Through an analysis of the NFA provisions relating to resources such as fish, timber, wildlife, and mines and minerals, I argue that the treaty moves beyond a fixed notion of Aboriginal culture, and instead reflects a recognition of culture as dynamic and performative. This acceptance of Aboriginal culture allows for the recognition of rights and powers beyond practices central to the Aboriginal culture prior to contact.

It will ultimately be argued that the uncomfortable nature of cultural negotiation in a postcolonial world is made manifest in this agreement, which results in the deep anxiety that the NFA evokes in both Aboriginal scholars and Canadian commentators. We as a society have to grapple with the question of whether Canadian law and politics should embrace and support the idea of strong modern First Nations, or whether Canadian tolerance is limited to protecting traditional expressions of First Nations culture until the only traces left are in climate-controlled exhibits in museums. If it is the former, then First Nations need the power to control and develop modern resources to compete in the global economy. If it is the latter, then either through extinction or assimilation First Nations culture may eventually be nothing more than a footnote in Western history.

Forest Resources

Forest resources have always been of great importance to the Nisga'a. Timber is necessary for building houses, smoking fish, heating, carving canoes, and creating ceremonial poles. Prior to the treaty, timber resources in the Nass Valley were considered to be Crown lands, and were licensed to companies by the provincial government for economic activities such as logging. These licences have historically resulted in ecological devastation in the Nass Valley. Under the NFA, timber resources on Nisga'a core lands are owned by the Nisga'a Nation. Timber resources on the balance of Nisga'a traditional territory are subject to power-sharing arrangements that provide the Nisga'a Lisims Government (NLG) with some control over forest resources and their management. This section will explore these arrangements with a view to understanding the fine balance between Nisga'a rights and Nisga'a power in the NFA. While timber is the resource that has been the most economically important in the Western economy, it should be noted that other forest resources are also considered in the treaty. These resources include berries, mushrooms, and other plant life used for food, medicine, and other purposes.

Chapter 5 of the NFA recognizes the Nisga'a Nation as the owner of all forest resources on Nisga'a core lands. This recognition generally means that, on Nisga'a Lands, timber and other resources are not only owned by the Nisga'a, but also managed by the Nisga'a. Therefore, much like in the discussion of

Nisga'a title to core lands, there is not simple ownership in a private dimension but also ownership in a radical title sense — the right to manage and control. The Ownership of Resources provision is as follows:

> 3. On the effective date, the Nisga'a Nation owns all forest resources on Nisga'a Lands.
> 4. Nisga'a Lisims Government has the exclusive authority to determine, collect, and administer any fees, rents, royalties, or other charges in respect of
>   a. non-timber forest resources on Nisga'a Lands;
>   b. timber resources referred to in paragraphs 20 and 21; and
>   c. after the transition period, all timber resources on Nisga'a Lands.[1]

Ownership, however, is not a very straightforward concept without more illustration. From a basic definition, it means: "The most far-ranging right *in rem* the law allows to a person: to deal with something to the exclusion of everyone else or of everyone except one or more designated people."[2]

This definition captures the core aspect of ownership that has been argued to define ownership — the right to exclude. As Merrill has argued,

> the right to exclude others is more than just "one more essential" constituent of property — it is the *sine qua non*. Give someone the right to exclude others from a valued resource, i.e., a resource that is scarce relative to the human demand for it, and you give them property. Deny someone the exclusion right and they do not have property.[3]

The Nisga'a, then, from a basic definitional standpoint, have the right to exclude others from the forest resources on their land.

If we look at the impact of the forestry industry on the Nass Valley in the latter half of the twentieth century, the right for the Nisga'a to exclude is of pre-eminent importance. As Raunet describes,

> From 1948 to 1964, Columbia Cellulose built up a total holding of 7284 square kilometers, more than a third of it on Nishga land. The pattern of its activity was typical of colonialist enterprise. Valleys and hills were clearcut; the timber was trucked on unpaved roads to Terrace on the Skeena or else floated down to the harbour of Prince Rupert, then sawed or transformed into pulp for export to the United States, Japan,

and Europe. At·first, Columbia Cellulose concentrated on the areas closest to the mills and the most accessible nearby districts. In the space of a few years it had created a barren no man's land around the town of Terrace and was having to venture farther and farther afield to keep its big plant supplied. After ten years logging the forests of the Kitsumkalum Tsimshian to the north of Terrace, the multinational subsidiary decided to enter the fiefdom of the Nass.[4]

The result of this foray was ecological devastation.[5] This dire situation had prompted the Nisga'a Tribal Council in 1976 to propose that the British Columbia government take over authority for logging in the area such that they could implement a sustainable forestry management plan. This authority was not given during the 70s, but instead became part of the negotiation process. The right to exclude is therefore a key power that allows the NLG to control the management of forest resources.

Section 4, chapter 5 of the NFA further elaborates on Nisga'a power and ownership over forest resources. This provision recognizes the NLG's exclusive authority to charge fees, rents, or licences to access forest resources. In this way, they now have the authority that the British Columbia government once did to grant logging licences. The effect of this is that the monetary benefits will not go to a national or global corporation, or the British Columbia government, but directly to the Nisga'a Nation.

Besides economically benefiting from logging on Nisga'a lands, the NLG also gains control over logging practices. The treaty recognizes the NLG's jurisdiction to "make laws in respect of the management of timber resources on Nisga'a Lands."[6] The substance of these laws is further defined in section 8, to include riparian management, cut block design and distribution, road construction, maintenance and deactivation, reforestation, soil conservation, biodiversity, fire management, logging methods and forest health. The only limitation contained in the treaty is that these standards must "meet or exceed forest standards established under forest practices legislation applicable to Crown land."[7] Nisga'a forest management standards must be at least as rigorous as provincial standards, but may be more stringent. This allows for the Nisga'a to enact laws to prevent environmental degradation that has previously affected the Nass valley.

There are also guidelines for how these standards should be compared. The treaty states that when evaluating Nisga'a forest standards as against provincial law, they should be "compared collectively,"[8] and will be "deemed to meet or exceed forest standards established under forest practices legislation applicable to Crown land, if they are no more intrusive to the environment than the forest standards applicable to Crown land established under forest practices legislation."[9] The treaty also recognizes the Nisga'a Lisims Government's jurisdiction to "make laws in respect of non-timber forest resources on Nisga'a Lands,"[10] subject to the same arrangements as timber resources. There is also a co-management provision that provides for the NLG and the province to "negotiate arrangements to achieve coordination and administrative efficiencies in respect of matters such as timber harvesting plans, road building, forest health concerns, forest fire detection and suppression, non-timber forest resources, and the protection of fisheries habitat."[11]

These provisions recognize the jurisdiction of the NLG to make laws regarding timber harvesting and ecological management. The only requirement written into this provision is that the NLG regulations have to "meet or exceed" current forest standards for Crown lands. These provisions would allow for much more stringent environmental regulation over timber harvest on Nisga'a lands, which could prevent further ecological devastation. It would, for example, be in the NLG's power to limit the practice of clear-cut logging, and promote selective tree harvesting.

An examination of how the equivalency provisions operate further demonstrates the balance of rights and power in the NFA. Section 8 states that the Nisga'a laws created must cover the enumerated subject areas that are covered in British Columbia forest practice legislation, and, again, that these laws will "meet or exceed forest standards established under forest practices legislation applicable to Crown land."[12] The Nisga'a are therefore competent to legislate and regulate forest management. So we have the exercise of self-government power. In other terms, the Nisga'a have self-government as long as they abide by the existing law. One may wonder what kind of self-government this really is.

Further analysis of these sections provides some insight into how this equivalency requirement serves Nisga'a goals. One does not have to look far into British Columbia forest practice legislation, regulation, and standards to begin to understand how difficult this provision could potentially be. In relation to "invasive" plants, for example there are three levels of government legislation and regulation. There is a section in the *Forest and Range Practice Act* (SBC 2002, c.69) that states:

47. A person carrying out a forest practice or a range practice must carry out measures that are

(a) specified in the applicable operational plan, or

(b) authorized by the minister to prevent the introduction or spread of prescribed species of invasive plant.

In the regulations authorized under this statute, there is a provision that mandates the following:

14. For the purpose of section 47 [invasive plants] of the Act, a woodlot license holder must, subject to section 78 (1), specify measures in the holder's woodlot license plan to prevent the introduction or spread of species of plants prescribed in the Invasive Plants Regulation, if the introduction or spread is likely to be the result of the holder's forest practices.[13]

Finally, there are recommended practice manuals such as the British Columbia Ministry of Forests "Invasive Alien Plants Program: Control Measure Standards for 2004."[14] What, then, are the Nisga'a required to have in their legislation? Is it a provision that states they may make regulations in regard to invasive plants? Is it that they need to have a provision making it mandatory that all forestry management plans submitted to them have a provision dealing with invasive plants? Or is it that they have to enact the substantive procedures dictated in the documents relating to the control of invasive plants? Or none of the former options, but a more broad equivalency that allows an entirely different approach to invasive plants?

In the face of these ambiguities, section 9 provides some guidance. It states that, in relation to the subject areas that the Nisga'a must address, such as biodiversity, which would seemingly cover alien invasive plants, the determination of equivalency "will be compared collectively."[15] This suggests that the Nisga'a need not create legislation that specifically deals with each of the enumerated areas, but instead can create regulations that, as long as they deal with the areas in some manner, will satisfy the equivalency requirement. In section 10, it states that NLG laws "will be deemed to meet or exceed forest standards established under forest practices legislation applicable to Crown land, if they are no more intrusive to the environment than the forest standards applicable to Crown land established under forest practices legislation."[16] This therefore means that NLG forestry laws will be judged on their substantive effect, rather than on procedural mechanisms. The NLG laws, then, will not be judged on having the appropriate procedural mechanisms that require substantive policy on forest regulation, but rather on whether the effect of the laws put in place is equivalent to the effect of the provincial standards. While the British Columbia government in the area of forestry has become far less lenient in relation to environmental standards, for many years this would not have been a hard bar to meet — as evidenced by the environmental impact from the logging on Nisga'a lands prior to the treaty.

While the treaty requires the Nisga'a to have equivalent standards, there is a great deal of scope as to how these are implemented. The Nisga'a have long been stewards of their land. The treaty may be written in Western legal terms, but it anticipates that the means by which the Nisga'a implement this stewardship may differ.

Section 11 provides an insight into how these stewardship rules differ rather radically from the basic regulation of Crown land. In section 11, this equivalency standard is specifically applied to non-timber forest resources on Nisga'a lands. This provision recognizes the NLG's ability to establish standards and to regulate the harvesting of non-timber resources on Nisga'a lands. While timber is an important resource in terms of external economic trade, there are many non-timber resources that are also of great importance to the Nisga'a, as is described in *The Land and Resources*:

> The plants of the Nass are another part of our riches. They provide a great variety of foods, as well as basic building materials, materials for canoe and totem pole construction, materials for the construction of nets and traps, tools, medicines, food storage materials, and the fire that kept people warm and dry, cooked foods, and helped to preserve the meat, fish, berries, and edible inner bark of hemlock, spruce and jack pine. . . . Food plants include many different types of berries, edible inner bark, the leaves, stems and roots.[17]

The Nisga'a have always had laws relating to the harvesting of berries and other plant resources in the Nass Valley. The importance of these resources is reflected in Nisga'a trespass laws. As Adam Nisyok (Saxgum Hiiggook) describes:

> If another woman went to another clan's ant'aahlkw first she was almost [always] killed; if she went there before the ones who own the ant'aahklw. When it was harvest time to be the first to pick whatever they had on their ant'aahlkw. After they were satisfied with their take, they then opened it to others.[18]

While a corporate entity such as Weyerhauser may value biodiversity as a matter of corporate image and government regulation, the range of non-timber resources that have value to the Nisga'a is likely to result in different forestry practices. What a logging company such as Weyerhauser views as valueless waste material, the Nisga'a view as an important resource.

Finally, section 12 anticipates the continuing co-operative relationship between the NLG and the provincial government. This provision states that the NLG and the provincial government may negotiate arrangements in order to coordinate in areas related to forest resources. These areas include things like road building, and fishery detection. This provision reflects a reality of "national" sovereignty and environmental issues that plagues most of the world. It is a fact that almost all matters of the environment that are national cannot be seen as ending at the boundaries of that nation's territory. Roads connect territories. Fisheries, particularly river and ocean fisheries, are not nicely isolated from the impact of the policies of the neighbouring territory. Therefore, in terms of traditionally defined political relations, this treaty is an inter-national treaty. The remarkable aspect of this provision is that it explicitly recognizes the importance of negotiation and coordination because of the inter-related nature of environmental and infrastructure concerns.

While on Nisga'a core lands the benefit of harvesting resources will flow to the Nisga'a, the treaty also comes with greater responsibility. Sections 17 to 29 deal with the harvesting allowances, which are to be in force during the transition period between the treaty's implementation and full handover to Nisga'a control. Sections 30 to 56 deal with operational plans and compliance enforcement during the transition period. This includes provisions relating to responsibilities in relation to things like fire control and health. Sections 57 to 61 provide for a transition of the responsibility for fire suppression and control to the Nisga'a Lisims Government. The treaty provides that the provincial government will be required to implement measures for fire suppression and control "to the same extent and in the same manner as it is responsible for the control and suppression of forest fires on Crown land elsewhere in British Columbia" and "using the same priority assessment" during the transitional period. This includes paying the costs for fires originating in the former Indian reserves in the Nass Valley.[19]

After the transition period, the NLG becomes responsible "for control and suppression of forest fires on Nisga'a Public Lands," fires on Nisga'a village lands, and on Nisga'a private lands.[20] This includes financial responsibility for the cost of a fire on these lands that,

a. originates on Nisga'a Public Lands and is caused by an act of God or an industrial user authorized by the Nisga'a Nation;

b. originates on Crown land and is caused by an act of God;

c. originates on private land and is caused by an act of God; or

d. originates on Nisga'a Village Lands or on Nisga'a Private Lands.

The Nisga'a Lisims Government takes over primary responsibility for the suppression of fires, which is an expensive endeavour. This needs to be seen in the context of broader finance-sharing agreements, however.[21]

The other context that needs to be considered to understand the effect of this provision is the complex constitutional division of powers in Canadian federalism. Indian lands are currently under the constitutional responsibility of the federal government.[22] This means that the federal government is responsible for fire prevention and suppression. As the federal government does not really have a standing fire-fighting force, the actual performance of these duties is usually in the hands of the province, backed by the fiscal contributions of the federal government. Section 59, therefore, transfers responsibility over fires on Indian lands to the provincial government after the transitional period. Sections 59 to 61 transition responsibility and, more importantly, cost for fighting forest fires between the provincial government and the Nisga'a government. The effect of this is to transfer the responsibility over an important task to the government that is closest and most affected by its successful operation.

Under the NFA the Nisga'a are no longer Indians under the Indian Act, and therefore come out from the umbrella of federal jurisdiction. The treaty was not simply a straightforward transfer of power, but instead was a process of the Nisga'a taking some powers and rights from the federal government, and some powers and rights from the provincial government. The reserves that were previously established in the Nass Valley were under federal jurisdiction; however, all the land surrounding the reserves was provincial lands. Arguably, the NFA creates a much more streamlined and less complex system of governance, with the NLG taking powers from both federal and provincial competency. The recognition of these governance powers, however, also makes the Nisga'a more responsible for certain things like the control of forest fires on Nisga'a Lands after the transition period. Indeed, the Nisga'a become liable for costs incurred in the course of fighting fires that originate on Nisga'a Lands. This does have positive aspects, however, as it guarantees Nisga'a jobs in firefighting. The issue is whether the NLG will have the financial resources to live up to its obligations, and what will happen if it does not.

Responsibility for expensive and laborious things like the fighting of fires is not often reflected in the idealistic struggles for self-determination or self-government. Unfortunately, along with the powers of sovereignty come the responsibilities of governance as well. Indeed, for certain advocates on the right of the political spectrum, this treaty achieves a goal that has long been sought — the end of the government's financial responsibility to Aboriginal people. Much of the ambiguity from within the Nisga'a people about their new status reflects the reality that "with great power," to use a popular culture reference, "comes great responsibility."[23]

While the forestry provisions are fairly comprehensive, mechanisms still exist where continuing negotiation is required. In chapter 5, s. 33 a mechanism fundamental to the operation of these transition provisions is created — the Forestry Transition Committee. This committee is to be established by the Nisga'a Nation and British Columbia, and "each will appoint one member to the committee."[24] This committee is given powers to modify and amend the requirements for forest development plans, licences or road use permits during the transition period. This means that, even though provincial laws are to apply to Nisga'a Lands, the Forestry Committee has discretion to modify these requirements during the transition period, thus introducing flexibility.

Thus far this section has described the NFA's treatment of forestry resources on Nisga'a lands. There is the matter, however, of the 18,000 square kilometres of Nisga'a traditional territory that are not now Nisga'a lands under the treaty. Indeed, the primary criticism of the treaty is the irreconcilable loss of these traditional lands.[25] As Chief Harry Nyce Sr. recognized, "Yes, the core lands are small but we have to start somewhere."[26] On lands outside Nisga'a lands there are a few provisions that do, however, include the Nisga'a in the development of forest resources. First, c. 5 s. 75 states that

Canada or British Columbia will provide the Nisga'a Nation, through the Joint Fisheries Management Committee and the Wildlife Committee, the information concerning forest development plans applicable to all or part of the Nass Area that is provided to the ministries or departments of Canada and British Columbia participating on those committees.

This provision by no means guarantees any participation or influence over these plans, but it at least recognizes that the NLG is an important stakeholder in development over the Nass Area.

There are also provisions that contemplate Nisga'a acquisition of forest tenures outside Nisga'a core lands. Sections 76 to 78 provide for the Nisga'a Nation to acquire forest tenures up to an "aggregate allowable annual cut of up to 150,000 sq m."[27] These acquisitions require the approval of the Minister of Forests, and are subject to the *Forest Act*.[28] This is not an unregulated discretion. The Minister of Forests will approve an acquisition if "there has been a public process, in accordance with Ministry policy on tenure transfers and corporate concentration, that identifies public interests in relation to those matters" and "the tenure or tenures contain terms and conditions that address local employment."[29] This provision, therefore, allows for the Nisga'a to develop forestry interests in the Nass Area if the proper procedures are undertaken. These provisions address another important issue in relation to the forestry business — local employment. Under past forest licences, corporations were under no requirement to have any concern about local job creation, but typically brought in outside employees. This provision is a reflection of an important consideration to the Nisga'a.

In traditional Nisga'a Ayuukhlw, timber resources were of fundamental significance both for survival and for ceremonial purposes. This is reflected in the treatment of timber in Nisga'a law. As described in *Ayuukhl Nisga'a Study: The Land and Resources*, Vol. IV,

> Some types of resources were treated differently [than others allocated and controlled by clans and chiefs]. The trees of an ango'oskw belonged to the wilp [house], but other people could request permission to use a tree for special purposes, such as a canoe or totem pole building. The owners would then expect to be paid back some for the use some time in the future, during a feast or other ceremony.[30]

The "common bowl" philosophy is apparent in these traditional laws. The "common bowl" philosophy is in very basic terms the notion that it is the valley that provides for the people of the Nass, and therefore the people of the Nass must share these resources among themselves and others who also come to live in the valley. Another house could request permission to use timber, but this must be recognized and compensated for. Under the current doctrine of Aboriginal rights, which only recognizes traditional practices that are essential to an indigenous culture prior to European contact, the court may recognize the "right" of the Nisga'a to harvest trees for ceremonial or traditional purposes, but may not recognize that the Nisga'a should have the power to determine how to utilize and share the commercial resources of their forest with their own people and others. Indeed, this right not only ultimately fails to recognize the connection that the Nisga'a have always had with the valley, it would also fail to provide the Nisga'a with meaningful ways to utilize their forest resources to survive in the contemporary world. While dug-out canoes and totem poles are an important part of traditional Nisga'a culture, they cannot define it.

The forest provisions in the treaty are by no means a complete victory for the Nisga'a. What the treaty does do is try to create a balance between the rights that the Supreme Court seems willing to recognize, and the power of self-determination that the Nisga'a have always internally maintained. It will likely be years before the ecological, social, legal, and cultural impact of this transfer of power over forest resources will be apparent. It does, however, present much different possibilities. The NFA brings the management of forest resources back into the hands of those who live in the Nass Valley. There is therefore great potential for better stewardship of resources that may prove to be of benefit for all.

Fisheries

In the previous section, the forest resource provisions were examined in order to demonstrate the balance that the treaty tries to create between the legal definition of Aboriginal rights and the Nisga'a control over necessary resources. Chapters 8 and 9 in the treaty deal with other resources fundamental to Nisga'a survival. These are the marine and land animals and birds that the Nisga'a share the Nass Valley with. These creatures have been, and continue to be, food sources for the people of the Nass. Through examining both these chapters of the treaty and how these resources have been dealt with, I argue that the treaty attempts to move beyond the limitations of a fixed traditional conception of Aboriginal rights to a more flexible structure that can account for the contemporary requirements of the Nisga'a Nation.

In the *Van der Peet*[31] case, the legal framework supplied by the Supreme Court for the recognition of Aboriginal rights only sustains claims to Aboriginal rights that were central to the Aboriginal society prior to European settlement. We saw that in *Van der Peet* a commercial fishery was not a concept that could be recognized under this rubric. This Aboriginal right therefore could not extend to catching and selling ten fish under an Indian food licence. Indeed, this colonial regulation of fishing has been a central and constant conflict in Aboriginal-Canadian relations. As Harris argues in *Fish, Law and Colonialism*,

> "There is no single Act in the whole of Canada that raises more problems between authorities and Indian people than the Fisheries Act." These comments of Judge Cunliffe Barnett in the British Columbia Provincial Court at Williams Lake in 1979 suggest the extent of the conflict that continues between Natives and the Canadian state over access to and control of fisheries. The law that surrounds fish, constructing particular fisheries, remains a principal site of conflict. The confrontation over the lobster fishery off the East Coast following the Supreme Court of Canada's *Marshall* decision reveals this all too clearly.[32]

Harris argues that the Canadian state, through the failure to recognize the "existence of . . . systems of Native management and resource allocation"[33] was an example of the law being wielded as an instrument of colonial domination. If we accept, as he argues, that the imposition of Dominion fishing (and hunting) regulation was indeed a manifestation of the law as colonialism, then the NFA is potentially an important manifestation of decolonization.

The provisions in the NFA relating to fish entitlements (chapter 8, section 1-6) delineates the ownership and authority over fish entitlements. It vests the Nisga'a Nation with fish entitlements, and specifies that these entitlements are inalienable. It also states the basic entitlement of "Nisga'a citizens [to] have the right to harvest fish and aquatic plants in accordance with this Agreement."[34] These rights are only limited by "measures that are necessary for conservation,"[35] and "legislation enacted for the purposes of public health or public safety."[36] The land that these rights may be exercised on extends to the full 26,000 square kilometres the Nisga'a traditionally claimed. Thus, while the core lands may only be ten per cent of traditional lands, fishing rights extend over almost 100 per cent of Nisga'a traditional territories.

As the experience with the east coast Canadian fisheries demonstrated,[37] fish are not an unlimited resource. The conservation and protection of fisheries is fundamentally important. Therefore, in the treaty, notwithstanding that Nisga'a fish entitlements are treaty rights, a Nisga'a fish allocation that is set out as a percentage of the total allowable catch has the same priority in fisheries management decisions as the remainder of the total allowable catch of that species harvested in recreational and commercial fisheries.[38]

This provision dictates that Nisga'a fishing allowances will not get priority in provincial or federal conservation decisions, as against non-Nisga'a allowances. These provisions recognize an inalienable Nisga'a right to certain fishery allocations, which looks favourable to the Nisga'a, yet does not make their allowances a priority against other competing fishery claims. Similar to the land provisions, then, we have the recognition of a Nisga'a entitlement balanced against by the claims of others to the land and resources.

The treaty has had a significant effect on Nisga'a participation in fisheries. In the 2008/2009 NFA Implementation Report, it is reported that $6,654,114 has entered the Nisga'a economy from the salmon harvest since 2000. When considering Van der Peet's entitlement to engage in commercial fisheries, this figure is impressive.

While salmon is an important species for the Nisga'a, there are many other species of fish and other aquatic life covered by the treaty. One significant fish is the oolichan, a small, greasy fish that appears in abundance around the spring equinox. These fish are important because of the time of year they emerge, and the high grease content.[39] As described by Chester Benson (Nit-slaganoo) in *The Land and Resources:*

At the end of winter, when the cedar boxes in which they store food are almost empty, it is the oolichan run in March that saves our people from starving. People then move up to Fishery Bay, which originally belonged to the Nisghas.[40]

Oolichan as well as salmon, seemingly as a result of their importance and their origin in the river, were considered common resources. As written in *The Land and Resources,* "all people were entitled to use the river for their harvests of salmon and oolichan and for travel. The oolichan were a common resource, since they spawned in the Nass."[41] It was not only the Nisga'a that were allowed to harvest oolichan, as neighbouring nations that were on good terms with the Nisga'a could also join in the harvest.[42]

Oolichan, not being a food generally consumed by anyone outside the

Nass Valley, did not require lengthy provisions in the treaty. The provisions that are included, however, do demonstrate how a colonial non-Aboriginal legal regime cannot properly anticipate the needs of Nisga'a law. In the NFA the only provisions relating to oolichan are the following:

> 62. The Nisga'a Nation, together with any other persons who have aboriginal rights to harvest oolichan in the Nass Area, has the right to harvest the total harvest of oolichan in the Nass Area.
> 63. If there are any agreements between the Nisga'a Nation and other aboriginal people in respect of the harvesting of oolichan in the Nass Area, Nisga'a harvests of those oolichan will be in accordance with those agreements.[43]

While the right to fish commercially viable fish such as salmon creates hot debate among non-Aboriginals, the fishing of oolichan, a resource specific to the Nisga'a and neighbouring Nations, is simply wholesale given to the Nisga'a. Apparently, if a resource is not a commodity there is very little concern over making it an entirely unregulated Aboriginal right.

In relation to the management of fisheries, there are aspects of both internal Nisga'a control and external Nisga'a participation contemplated in the treaty. Ultimately, "the Minister is responsible for the management of fisheries and fish habitat."[44] The Nisga'a, however, have jurisdiction over aspects of internal distribution of fishery entitlements, registration of fishing vessels, administration of license requirements, and regulation of sales of fish so long as these laws are not inconsistent with Nisga'a annual fishing plans.

This co-operative jurisdiction is required because fisheries, and particularly salmon fisheries involving other spawning species, cannot be regulated solely within national boundaries. The treaty creates two major mechanisms for the Nisga'a to participate in the external regulation of fishing. The first is the Joint Fisheries Management Committee, which is created as a mechanism for the joint participation in decision making. This committee is a vehicle for the sharing of information regarding fisheries that are the basis for the yearly general allocations. The treaty also creates the Lisims Fisheries Conservation Trust, which is a body created to "promote conservation and protection of Nass Area fish species," "facilitate sustainable management of fisheries for Nass Area species and stocks," and "promote and support Nisga'a participation in the stewardship of Nass Area fisheries for the benefit of all Canadians."[45] Within the treaty, the federal government pledged ten million dollars, and the Nisga'a pledged three million dollars for the establishment and operation of these objects. In addition, in relation to fisheries, there is one of the few provisions in the treaty that expressly contemplates Nisga'a consultation on international policy in relation to fisheries.[46]

The success of the structure that the NFA creates in relation to fisheries is best judged by experts in the area. A 2006 article provides an indication of how this structure is working:

Nass Salmon Fishery Gets Top Marks
Ottawa, Aug 09, 2006

An in-depth study of the salmon fisheries of British Columbia's Nass River has earned top marks for Canada's federal government and for the Nisga'a government, which co-manages the fishery with Ottawa.

"This is probably as good as it gets in salmon fisheries management," says report author David Levy, one of Canada's top salmon biologists.

The Nass River Salmon Fishery Report Card, released today by the Sierra Club of Canada, gives the fishery an overall grade of "B." A key feature of the fishery is a stock assessment system that Levy judges to be one of the best of any salmon fishery in the world.[47]

While creating effective systems of co-management can be challenging, the shared responsibility over Nisga'a fisheries seems to be effective. As the above article describes,

For years, we were told that the Nisga'a treaty would be a disaster for the Nass River salmon fisheries. This clearly proves the critics were wrong. . . . The Nisga'a and their partners in the federal government have set a fine example for what could be undertaken up and down B.C.'s coast.[48]

In comparison to the judicial determination of Aboriginal fishing rights, the NFA is a remarkably broad recognition of Nisga'a Aboriginal rights. The treaty provides for a substantial commercial allocation, as well as recognizing personal Aboriginal use. The treaty also provides for both the provincial and federal government to give 5.75 million dollars to the Nisga'a to "to enable it to increase its capacity, in the form of commercial licenses, or vessels and commercial licenses, to participate in the general commercial fishery in British Columbia."[49] This money has been used to allow Nisga'a members to purchase commercial fishing licences. These fishery provisions are not a reflection of a "frozen rights" approach to Aboriginal entitlement, but a recognition of the Nisga'a Nation as an important economic and conservation partner in the broader provincial and Canadian context. Traditional fishing practices and patterns such as the oolichan harvest are contained in the treaty, but the entire package is about contemporary Nisga'a participation in fisheries, not about simply retaining historical uses.

Wildlife and Migratory Birds

Fisheries may play a central role in Nisga'a life, but other animals and birds are also dealt with in the treaty (Chapter 9). Similar to the fisheries chapter, the treaty provides the Nisga'a with "the right to harvest wildlife throughout the Nass Wildlife Area in accordance with this Agreement subject to: measures that are necessary for conservation, and legislation enacted for the purposes of public health or public safety."[50] The territory over which they exercise this right is called the Nass Wildlife Area and comprises approximately 16,000 square kilometres. This entitlement is describes in section 2 as the "right to harvest in a manner that . . . is consistent with . . . the communal nature of the Nisga'a harvest for domestic purposes, and . . . the traditional seasons of the Nisga'a harvest and does not interfere with other authorized uses of Crown land."[51] This right is described in relation to Nisga'a traditional uses and practices, but is limited by the provision that it not interfere with other Crown uses of the land. In a later section, the treaty states that, aside from some exceptions, "Nisga'a wildlife allocations are for domestic purposes."[52] Essentially, what this entitlement creates is the right for Nisga'a to procure wildlife and migratory birds from the Nass Wildlife Area without the federal or provincial government's rules of general application, such as requiring a licence, to apply.[53] Outside the Nass Wildlife Area however, rules of general application will apply — even on lands owned in fee simple by Nisga'a outside this area.[54]

Much like fisheries, however, the general Aboriginal right to harvest wildlife, even on Nass Wildlife Area lands, is constrained in certain ways by allowable harvests for designated species. Section 15 initially designates moose, grizzly bear, and mountain goat as designated species that will be subject to total harvest allowances to address problems of species facing "significant risk."[55] These designations can be removed by the Minister if the "significant risk no longer exists."[56] In determining the total allowable harvests of designated species, the Minister "will request and consider recommendations from the Wildlife Committee before determining the total allowable harvest."[57] The criteria defined in the treaty that the Minister must base his or her allocations on are also defined, being the population of these species both within the Nass Wildlife Area, as well as the population of "species within its normal range of area of movement outside the Nass Wildlife Area."[58] In the case of a dispute over the total allowable harvest of designated species, or the designation of such species, the agreement includes an arbitration provision.

The responsibilities and powers of the Nisga'a in relation to wildlife are similar to those in relation to fisheries. While the Minister ultimately has the responsibility to manage the harvesting of wildlife both in the Nass Wildlife Area and outside, the creation of management plans is done according to the process defined in the treaty, making it a joint endeavour. The Nisga'a, though, have the jurisdiction to "make laws that are in respect of the Nisga'a Nation's rights and obligations in respect of wildlife and migratory birds under, and that are consistent with this Agreement and that are not inconsistent with the annual management plans."[59] The areas in the treaty that are contemplated by this provision include licensing, the control of methods and seasons of harvest, and the regulation of any trade or barter under wildlife entitlements.[60] The Nisga'a also have the responsibility, as this provision is made in mandatory language, to "require: a. that any wildlife or wildlife parts, including meat, harvested under this Agreement, that are transported outside Nisga'a Lands for the purpose of trade or barter be identified as wildlife for trade or barter; and . . . Nisga'a citizens to comply with the annual management plan."[61] Therefore, embedded in these provisions are both non-mandatory jurisdictional powers and mandatory regulatory requirements.

While the provisions described above are all related to the domestic and personal use of wildlife resources, there are a few exceptions in the treaty that contemplate the commercial sale of wildlife and migratory birds. In chapter 9, sections 70 and 92, it merely states that any sale of wildlife parts or migratory birds will be done "in accordance with federal and provincial laws of general application, and with any Nisga'a law in respect of sale of wildlife."[62] The other provision is found in section 93, which states that "Nisga'a citizens have the right to sell inedible by-products, including down, of migratory birds harvested under this Agreement."[63]

There are other specific issues addressed in the wildlife and migratory birds chapter that have great economic importance to the Nisga'a. This is the ownership of traplines, and the holding of licences for guiding. The ownership of traplines has always been an important land-based right to the Nisga'a. If one were to make a comparison to common law property constructs, a trapline could be compared to an exclusive *profit a prendre*. *Profit a prendre*, in property law, is the right to enter and remove something from the land. A trapline — or a hunting ground or berry patch, for that matter — was held by a clan and fiercely protected. As Adam Nisyok (Saxum Hiiggook) describes,

> [With] mountain goats, for example, one would go and keep checking the[m]. He would kill one, check the flesh. When the tallow is thick, it is ready. Then the hunting begins. . . . Once again, the trapping/hunting ground is opened to others afterward. And if someone else went there first he was killed.[64]

The severity of the trespass laws demonstrates the importance of this territorially based right. In the treaty, however, this right does not appear in the land chapter, but in the wildlife chapter. This illustrates an interesting point about how the NFA was constructed. The variety and scope of the specific entitlements that are important to the Nisga'a cannot be easily reflected in a simple translation to common law principles. Theoretically, if the Nisga'a were given all the powers of a sovereign nation state within their entire historical territory, then all these entitlements, practices, and rights that the Nisga'a find important could be actualized. Because the treaty describes the modified rights of the Nisga'a Nation, attention to all aspects of life important to the Nisga'a had to be negotiated into the treaty.

Trapping and guiding, however, are not only of economic consequence to the Nisga'a. but are a matter of general concern in British Columbia. There are provincial laws applying to the granting and licensing of traplines and guiding. As the Ministry of Environment has described:

> Trapping is a recognized and long-standing use of wildlife in British Columbia. First Nations have trapped wildlife for thousands of years, and trapping and fur-trading played a significant role in the exploration and early development of B.C. by European settlers. The Province's first trapping regulations were established in 1906 in an effort to conserve the province's fur-bearing animals. Fur royalties were first imposed in

1921 and continue today and the Province began registering traplines in 1925 to reduce disputes among trappers and provide security for investment in trails and trapline shelters. Currently, there are over one thousand licensed trappers in B.C. Trapping continues to be an important activity for some First Nations and the owners of registered traplines, however, its economic significance has greatly declined as consumer demand for fur clothing has decreased.[65]

Guiding is also an important economic activity and is regulated through provincial legislation enacted in 1948.[66] This is a more relevant contemporary activity, as it is a part of the very lucrative tourism industry. Guiding provides tourists with the opportunity to engage in activities such as big-game hunting, wildlife viewing, and trail rides.

The treaty provisions in the NFA transfer the ownership of traplines and guiding permits that are wholly or partially connected to Nisga'a Lands to the Nisga'a Nation if they are not registered to a person, or if they become abandoned. Similarly, if a guiding licence is abandoned, a licence will be granted to the Nisga'a Nation. Also, before the government issues any new trapline licences or guiding licences connected to their land, the Nisga'a will be consulted. In relation to this matter, it is one of the many provisions that is still to be negotiated. Section 77 states,

> British Columbia and the Nisga'a Nation will negotiate and attempt to reach agreement in respect of Nisga'a Lisims Government authority for the management of some or all of traplines that are registered to the Nisga'a Nation, a Nisga'a Village, a Nisga'a Institution, a Nisga'a Corporation, or Nisga'a citizens, in the Nass Wildlife Area.[67]

This in one of the areas of the treaty that demonstrate that it is not a completed process, but one that will continue, based on the grounding of the procedures and principles that the NFA stands for.

Mines and Minerals

At the time of European settlement in North America, there was another category of resources that was not contemplated which now forms a part of Nisga'a entitlement in the treaty. Indeed, one wonders if the abandonment of British claims over Canadian territory would have happened so easily if there had been foreknowledge of both the importance of oil in the modern world, and Canada's abundance in this resource. The right to own and control the mines and mineral wealth on Aboriginal land, then, clearly does not fall under a claim for an Aboriginal right. The claim to ownership of this resource is based upon a much broader claim. Mineral resources are therefore contained in the land chapter of the treaty.

In the NFA, minerals are defined as "ores of metal and all natural substances that can be mined," including "rock or other materials from mine tailings, dumps, and previously mined deposits of minerals," and "coal, petroleum, gas, earth, soil, peat, marl, sand, gravel, rock, stone, limestone, dolomite, marble, shale, clay, volcanic ash, and diatomaceous earth," and "all precious and base minerals."[68] This definition includes all the commercially important resources that are potentially located on Nisga'a Lands. More importantly, though, the Nisga'a gain the exclusive power to "determine, collect, and administer any fees, rents, royalties, or other charges in respect of mineral resources on or under Nisga'a Lands."[69] While there is no provision that expressly contemplates the Nisga'a Lisims Government's ability to stop any oil or mineral exploration on Nisga'a Lands, they could make it not economically viable for this type of development to occur by charging exorbitant royalties. It is contemplated, however, that the province could expropriate mineral interests.[70] A higher standard of justification for expropriation, however, also applies to Nisga'a Lands. The cumulative effect of these provisions does provide the Nisga'a greater control over whether mineral resources get developed at all, and provide them with the revenue from these resources if they are.

Conclusion

In chapter one, I argued that postcolonial theory encourages one to examine culture as a living, evolving dynamic group of practices rather than a fixed list of historic practices. The Nisga'a Final Agreement demonstrates this different model of cultural recognition through recognizing Nisga'a management over all the resources that have been important to them in the past, but also the resources that are important in the present, and in the future. This reflects a different understanding of culture that is performative, rather than fixed. Through analyzing the NFA provisions on forest resources, fisheries, wildlife and migratory birds, and mines and minerals, this chapter has demonstrated how the NFA not only recognizes the Nisga'a right to resources, but the power of the Nisga'a to share in the management of these resources. This chapter therefore demonstrates that the treaty develops hybrid rights that are located somewhere between rights and power. This hybridity ultimately evades the static, and ultimately detrimental, "frozen rights" approach that still dominates Canadian jurisprudence. While the jurisprudential recognition of Aboriginal rights has been predicated upon the recognition of Aboriginal practices that were "of central significance to the aboriginal society in question,"[71] the NFA attempts to secure access and control over the key resources that are fundamental to the Nisga'a Nation's social and economic viability. It is through this viability in the contemporary world that Nisga'a cultural life can flourish in the future.

The resource provisions of the NFA evade an essentialist definition of Aboriginal rights through finely balancing Aboriginal rights with Aboriginal powers. An Aboriginal right, the way the Supreme Court has defined it, is a conception of a right that is ultimately bounded by its source and its interpretation. These rights are sourced in the "ancient occupation and use of land,"[72] and therefore their modern manifestations are irrevocably frozen in the distant past. Through construing these rights as narrowly as possible, the court has further eviscerated any potential that the jurisprudential determination of rights can provide.

The NFA, however, has not escaped criticism. These criticisms tend to focus on the land provisions rather than on a more holistic look at all the recognized entitlements in the treaty — which may be why these criticisms may not be as accurate as they could be. Rynard, for example, writes that "the agreement compromises and limits Nisga'a land rights in ways that suggest that too little progress has been made since Canada announced in 1973 that it was willing to negotiate treaties with First Nations."[73] In his recommendations for future treaties, he again emphasizes the failure of the treaty in relation to full recognition of Nisga'a entitlement to land. He urges that "subsequent negotiations should demand far fewer concessions, particularly concerning land rights, or the just and mutually beneficial reconciliation envisioned by the Royal Commission on Aboriginal Peoples (RCAP) will remain out of reach."[74] Rynard concludes that if this pattern of Canadian legal inflexibility continues, reconciliation with First Nations "will likely not be possible because agreements and treaties will either be unreachable or be tainted as coerced surrenders."[75]

Rynard's critique focuses primarily on the land provisions of the treaty. If one views land rights narrowly, the treaty does indeed seem rather bleak. If one views the treaty more holistically, however, there is a complex package of rights and powers that fairly comprehensively address all the resources important to the Nisga'a. This narrow focus is demonstrative of the treaty's attempt to balance the liberal recognition of pre-contact Indigenous culture and the postcolonial recognition of powers essential to Nisga'a culture. There is no surrender of rights, just a recognition of powers within the Canadian governmental system. It is unsurprising that this recognition is not one of complete sovereignty, but a complex negotiation of jurisdiction. It is unsurprising because the Nisga'a were not negotiating for independence; they were negotiating for the power to control the resources important for their nation.

The NFA recognizes entitlements and jurisdictions that go far beyond the core lands. The strength of the Nisga'a Nation's position in these co-management structures is currently very hard to evaluate. I would argue, however, that there is a deep-seated problem with the foundation of critiques such as Rynard's. This critique, as articulated by Macklem, is that the Canadian legal system has not yet come to terms with "native difference."[76] He writes that "each frame of reference utilized by the law . . . to structure and make sense of native disputes . . . perpetuates a legal relationship of dependency by native peoples on the Canadian state."[77] Ultimately, though, there will always be an inter-dependence between the NLG, the province, and the federal government. The question is not whether native difference is recognized; it is how the ongoing relations between the Nisga'a, the province, and the federal government honour native difference. The NFA makes the NLG independent of the Canadian state in many respects. It seems that critics of the treaty are ultimately worried that this independence is not tenable.

I fear that the underlying assumption about Aboriginal culture underlining these perspectives is still ultimately predicated upon the fixed and essentialist understanding of Aboriginal culture. Admittedly, the discourse of prior occupation has been a powerful one in Canadian jurisprudence, but this discourse is problematic in a contemporary context. Both Macklem and Rynard assume that native difference is and should be understood and recognized as a radical "other" to the Canadian legal system. If not, it seems they are arguing that Aboriginal peoples are still being fleeced into assimilation and dependency. The Nisga'a seem, however, to identify their culture in a modern context, not as a reflection of some essentialist Nisga'a cultural criteria. This is not to say that the use of a Western legal framework is without its problems. It is this framework, however, that was a tool they could use to secure both their place in the Canadian political community, and the resources so essential to the economic and social viability of their communities.

◌

CHAPTER FOUR

Power

Introduction

If you read any of the major reports published on First Nations in Canada, they seem to tacitly accept that Aboriginal self-government is an essential aspect of reconciliation.[1] Since the 1990s, however, the discourse has shifted from governance toward rights. The simmering discontent expressed by First Nations that seems to erupt occasionally across Canada cannot, however, be addressed by rights. Let us take as an example the development of the oil sands in northern Alberta. The criticisms one reads of oil sand development is that, despite First Nations' established treaty rights, resource development continues to overrun their traditional territory. Chief Rick Horseman has explained:

> To date, it's been like watching a game of musical chairs where everyone is saying they are addressing our concerns, rights and interests but no one actually gets down to it and does it. We need a referee in Alberta that will deal with First Nations in a serious and impartial way and blow the whistle when our rights are being trampled.[2]

Clearly, some power or authority is required to enforce meaningful considera-tion of First Nation concerns about the decisions that affect their rights. Even if a First Nation has rights to a pristine area of treaty land, if it is surrounded by strip mines there needs to be a meaningful way for First Nations to have their interests protected.

This chapter will therefore explore the meaning of sovereignty, self-deter-mination, and self-government in the NFA. I will examine a possible version of First Nation sovereignty within the state of Canada that is premised upon rights, but extends these right to the power for Indigenous peoples of Canada to make decisions about their future both on and off their treaty lands. This is a concept of sovereignty that can operate within the sovereign Canadian state, rather than in a Western conception of exclusive "national" sovereignty. I will then argue that the constitution of the Nisga'a Lisims Government in the governance provisions, as well as some of the primary jurisdictions of the NLG such as education and administration of justice, reflect an overlapping and fluid postcolonial conception of sovereignty.

This chapter will ultimately argue that the treaty, while not creating a new "sovereign" Nisga'a Nation in Western terms, does provide the NLG with the power and jurisdiction to create a legal framework that both internally reflects Nisga'a cultural practices, and externally provides them with the ability to participate in the greater Canadian political community. This participation constitutes a significant move toward decolonization, as it allows the Nisga'a Lisims Government to be an active and recognized political and legal force within Canadian society. While it will become clear that there are administrative and structural difficulties that hamper this participation, the framework in the treaty does achieve the basic recognition of the Nisga'a as partners in Canada's future, rather than simply a historical anomaly of a colonial past.

The Nisga'a Nation: Sovereignty, Self-Determination, and Self-Government

Before embarking on an analysis of the NFA, it is important to first make an attempt to grapple with the meaning of sovereignty, self-determination, and self-government in a broader context. These are all contentious terms laden with layers of meaning — and, I would argue, misunderstanding. In order to move toward a common understanding of these terms, this section will compare some Western conceptions of sovereignty with some Canadian discourse on Aboriginal sovereignty. While in Western political and legal theory, sovereignty is not an uncontested notion, it will become apparent that there are some general aspects of sovereignty that are inconsistent with Canadian Aboriginal discourse on what First Nation sovereignty means. It is not the goal of this section to comprehensively explore a "Western" notion of sovereignty, but simply to highlight how the general genealogy of sovereignty, vis-à-vis a few of the influential theorists on sovereignty, differs from a First Nation perception.

Sovereignty, in Western political theory, is a difficult term to define. As Raia Prokhovnik has written, "[e]ach theory of sovereignty focuses upon a different cluster of general features, attributes, marks, properties, and conditions to define and indicate the location and meaning of sovereignty, and no theory includes them all."[3] Within this diversity, however, there is a general concern with authority and legitimacy. Alain de Benoist has described the general preoccupation with sovereignty as having a dual dimension:

> Usually sovereignty is defined in one of two ways. The first definition applies to supreme public power, which has the right and, in theory, the capacity to impose its authority in the last instance. The second definition refers to the holder of legitimate power, who is recognized to have authority. When national sovereignty is discussed, the first definition applies, and it refers in particular to independence, such as the freedom of a collective entity to act. When popular sovereignty is discussed, the second definition applies and sovereignty is associated with power and legitimacy.[4]

This concern with authority is prevalent in many of the influential thinkers on sovereignty. In Hobbes's *Leviathan,* sovereignty is "to confer all their power and strength upon one man or upon one assembly of men, that they may reduce all their wills by plurality of voices unto one will."[5] This single will in its purposes is to "conform the wills of them all to peace at home and mutual aid against their enemies abroad."[6] Considering Hobbes's opinion of the "natural condition of mankind as concerning their felicity and misery,"[7] it is not really surprising that he formulates sovereignty in such a manner. Indeed, he is of the opinion that "during the time men live without a common power to keep them all in awe, they are in that condition which is called war; and such a war, as is of every man against every man."[8] Therefore, the vesting of the sovereign with this power to conform all wills into a unified purpose seems important if one is not to live in such an unsettled and violent state. In Hobbes, it is God that is the legitimating force behind such a formulation of sovereignty, as it is by God's authority that the sovereign may act.

In Bodin, we get a similar concern with centralized authority. In chapter 8, Bodin defines sovereignty as "supreme power over citizens and subjects unrestrained by the laws."[9] As Benoist describes,

> Thus, Bodin's sovereignty is totally exclusive: giving the king the role of unique legislator, it grants to the state an unlimited and original authority. Consequently, a sovereign state is defined as one whose prince does not depend upon anyone but himself. This implies that a nation

is formed within a state, and that it is identified with this state. For Bodin, a country might be defined in terms of its history, its culture, its identity, or its morals, but politically, what constitutes a state as such is its sovereignty. Sovereignty is the absolute power that forms the republic as a political entity, unique and absolute. The state must be one and indivisible, because it represents the legislative monopoly of the sovereign. Local autonomies are allowed, but only if they do not constrain the authority of the prince. Therefore, they are always more limited. The state is a monad, while the prince is "separated from the people." i.e., placed in an isolation bordering on solipsism.[10]

Sovereignty, in both Hobbes and Bodin, is an expression of a centralized unified supreme power set apart and above the masses.

While Hobbes and Bodin express sovereignty as an absolute unqualified power that is only abstractly justified by a "social contract,"[11] Locke and Rousseau "[b]oth take the idea of a social contract seriously."[12] There is therefore more of a concern about legitimacy. While Locke and Rousseau both present a rather different version of sovereignty, their theoretical reliance on a notion of popular sovereignty is similar. Despite this concern with "consent" and sovereign legitimacy, however, Aboriginal people were excluded. As Ivison has argued,

> Locke, for example, is said to have thickened out the anthropological minimalism grounding man's natural freedom with socio-cultural conceptions of rational competency and "reasonableness" that rules out taking the claims of Indigenous peoples seriously. His conception of property, and what constituted a proper "political society," are elaborated with reference to specific set of European assumptions which conveniently delegitimated Native American sovereignty and landholding practices.[13]

Rousseau disagreed with Hobbes's view of the state of nature, and instead romanticized the "noble savage."[14] In Rousseau's account, however, sovereignty is "inalienable and indivisible."[15] In addition, a sovereign act "binds and favours all citizens equally, so that the sovereign recognizes only the whole body of the nation and makes no distinction between the members who compose it."[16] Popular sovereignty therefore legitimizes the expression of a unified sovereign authority.

In the work of Carl Schmitt, we see an attempt to describe sovereignty in a level of "concrete application." This is where we see the emergence of the statement that "sovereign is he who decides the exception."[17] He writes:

> From a practical or theoretical perspective, it really does not matter whether an abstract scheme advanced to define sovereignty (namely, that sovereignty is the highest power, not derived power) is acceptable. About an abstract concept there will in general be no argument, least of all in the history of sovereignty. What is argued about is the concrete application, and that means who decides in a situation of conflict what constitutes the public interest or interest of state, public safety and order, *le salut* public and so on. The exception, which is not codified in the existing legal order, can at best be characterized as a case of extreme peril, a danger to the existence of the state, or the like. But it cannot be circumscribed factually and made to conform to a performed law.[18]

We therefore have here a criterion for sovereignty, a test to avoid the abstract notional definitions of sovereignty. The enunciation of this notion of sovereignty implicitly recognizes that the "sovereign" may not always be who he claims to be. It is not a question of who has the theoretical legitimacy to be sovereign, or even the apparent authority, but instead the question is who actually has the power to decide.

In a constitutionally federal state such as Canada, this test becomes rather meaningless on a practical plane. In a time of emergency it is the federal government that is sovereign and decides the exception under the *Emergencies Act*.[19] As Canada has an entrenched Charter, however, even decisions made under such measures are subject to judicial review. If the government does not agree with a ruling of the Supreme Court, they then have recourse to the notwithstanding clause (clause 33) which will allow an Act to stand notwithstanding the provisions of the Charter. This provision mandates, however, that every five years clause 33 has to be reinvoked. The exception no longer seems to be a meaningful test under existing Canadian law. According to Schmitt's criteria, the sovereign is a rather fluid notion in the Canadian constitutional structure.

Even in relation to more mundane matters, Canadian federalism does not lend itself to a fixed notion of sovereignty. Section 91 and 92 of the Canadian Constitution divide areas of legislative competency between federal and provincial powers. To answer the question of who decides the exception, one looks to what legislative area the emergency falls under. This does not mean, however, that Schmitt's notion of the sovereign exception is meaningless as a gauge for sovereign power, just that the power to decide is fairly comprehensively determined by the Canadian Constitution. Indeed, this may be a very good test to explore whether Aboriginal peoples in Canada generally, and particularly the Nisga'a under the NFA, are exercising sovereign power. If the Nisga'a have competency to decide the exception in any areas, it would seem fair to describe the Nisga'a Nation, at least to the extent of that power, as sovereign. Aboriginal governance will therefore be examined based on Schmitt's notion of the sovereign.

Articulations of Aboriginal sovereignty in Canadian discourse are also tempered by the federal nature of Canadian constitutionalism. As Erasmus and Sanders write,

> We don't want to scare Canadians with our terminology. No one is scared in this country by the fact that Ontario or Manitoba can make laws in education and not a single power in the world can do anything about it. They are sovereign in their area of jurisdiction. We, likewise, want to have clear powers over our territories.
>
> Canada is already set up for it, because we have a confederation that lends itself very easily to what our people are asking for. We have the federal government, we have federal powers. We have provinces, we have provincial powers. We have some areas where the two overlap. We could easily have a third list of First Nation powers.[20]

Aboriginal sovereignty is not, therefore, in this formulation, about absolute independence from the state. It is about garnering jurisdictional powers over aspects of government important to the survival of First Nations within the Canadian state. In an interview with the president of the Nisga'a Lisims Government, Nelson Leeson, this understanding of Aboriginal sovereignty was enunciated. He underlined that sovereignty is often seen as independence from the existing state, rather than participation within it. He said that sovereignty to the Nisga'a was not about independence: the "Nisga'a wanted to make decisions about our own lives, but wanted to be a part of Canada. It was about determining our own destiny."[21] He also was of the opinion that "sovereignty is not about separation; it is exciting to get more responsibility."[22] The treaty, in his view, was therefore a mechanism whereby the Nisga'a could make decisions about their own lives and resources within the Canadian state, rather than a desire to be separate from the state. In his words, "the game is to get out of the cycle of dependency. The NFA is set out to do that."[23]

The goal of Aboriginal sovereignty is not therefore separation from Canada, but a partnership within it. As Ed Wright described, the Nisga'a always "had sovereignty but had to find a way to express it." He stated:

> People think that if you recognize the sovereignty of the Crown you abandon your own sovereignty — this is just not true. If you can get Canada to sit down with you then it means that they recognize you are sovereign. When you sign a treaty that also recognizes your sovereignty. Waving the sovereignty flag for the means of getting in someone's face doesn't work.[24]

Wright therefore sees no contradiction between recognizing Canadian sovereignty and maintaining Nisga'a sovereignty. Under the agreement, as a nation they are, seemingly, being externally recognized, whereas before they were not.

Aboriginal sovereignty is therefore bound up with what Michael Asch has called "political self-sufficiency." This involves rooting Aboriginal government within the existing Canadian constitutional framework, without it being controlled by it. As Asch writes,

> Political self-sufficiency means, at its most basic level, having the ability to set goals and to act on them without seeking permission from others. When looked at in this way, it is clear that Canada has consistently denied political self-sufficiency to aboriginal nations. . . .
>
> Political self-sufficiency for aboriginal peoples in Canada means not only through acquiring certain political and economic resources through negotiations with the federal and provincial governments; it also means acquiring these resources in a manner that is free from both symbols and reality of dependency.[25]

For the Nisga'a Nation this does seem to have been the goal — the ability to make decisions about their communities rather than being subject to the paternal administrations of the Indian Act bureaucracy.

On a very basic level, this has been denied to the Nisga'a under the *Indian Act*.[26] As Deanna Nyce described, when the water supply for Gitwinksihlkw became contaminated, the village made plans to use the Nass river, which flows right by the village, as a source of water. These plans were submitted to the *Indian Act* administrative system, but were placed among the many requests for reserve improvements. The village, as a result, had to truck in clean water for several years. Simple ownership rights, from a Western perspective, could not provide the power for the village to be able to address these issues themselves. If, however, Nisga'a title also provides jurisdictional powers, no outside government agency is directly required for the development of a clean water supply. It is true that, under the treaty, standard provincial and federal environmental regulations would apply to projects such as this. The difference is that, rather than being placed in a queue for Indian projects across Canada by a bureaucrat in Ottawa, the Nisga'a village could press forward without previous approvals. Even in a complex global society, it is difficult to see how abiding by national or international regulations is antithetical to recognizing some form of sovereignty. If this were the case, no Western nation subject to internationally agreed treaties would be sovereign.

There are aspects of the bureaucracy for administering the *Indian Act* that create obstacles to the full participation of the Nisga'a in government. It was mentioned by several members of the government that, despite Nisga'a status as a self-governing entity with jurisdictional competence over quite a few areas, their participation is still being channeled through the existing *Indian Act* bureaucracy. As Kevin MacKay described, the "Crown have not realized the need for a sole department to implement treaties, instead they have seconded the INAC (Indian and Northern Affairs Canada) to implement treaties."[27] This use of INAC as the mechanism for implementation of treaty rights was identified as being at the heart of the failure of the provincial and federal governments to fulfill their obligations in the treaty. While negotiating the treaty, the Nisga'a dealt with ministers and high-level civil servants. After the negotiations, implementation was handled by the existing INAC bureaucracy. With the number of comprehensive land claims and self-government agreements increasing, however, this haphazard arrangement for implementation may indeed be forced to change.

The discourse on Aboriginal sovereignty, therefore, points to a notion of sovereignty that would, seemingly, fall under Schmitt's test of the sovereign exception in a limited way. The discourse of Aboriginal sovereignty in Canada is about having the power to decide the exception, but only over those aspects of government competency that fall under the jurisdiction agreed to through reasonable negotiation with the provincial and federal government. This notion of sovereignty is internally focused — concerned with internal decision making. Indeed, as Kevin Mackay stated, "we don't want a seat in the UN between Nigeria and Swaziland, we are happy to have Canada do those things"[28]

Nisga'a Lisims Government: Structure and Constitution

In this section, the status of the Nisga'a Final Agreement within Canadian law, as well as the basic constitution of Nisga'a government structures, will be explored. I argue that, while the Canadian state has generally refused to recognize Aboriginal sovereignty, the NFA recognizes the limited sovereign power of the Nisga'a Lisims Government within the terms negotiated in the treaty. Through analyzing the provisions that govern the relationship of the NLG to the provincial and federal governments, I will demonstrate how a balance is being struck between Canadian "sovereignty" and Nisga'a internal "self-determination." Similar to the provisions on Nisga'a core lands, the treaty creates a hybrid between Aboriginal rights and sovereign powers, which in turn creates a tension between the constitutional sovereignty of the Canadian state and the recognition of Nisga'a sovereignty.

There are several provisions that together can be read as establishing the legal status of the agreement. Chapter 2, section 1 states that the NFA is "a treaty and a land claims agreement within the meaning of sections 25 and 35 of the Constitution Act, 1982." This means that the NFA is sheathed with the constitutional protection afforded by these sections.[29] Section 35 constitutionally recognizes and affirms Aboriginal and treaty rights. Subsection 35(3) clarifies that this protection "includes rights that now exist by way of land claims agreements or may be so acquired." Section 25 of the Constitution (1982) ensures that the *Canadian Charter of Rights and Freedoms* is not interpreted as to "abrogate or derogate" from constitutional protections of Aboriginal and treaty rights as existed in the *Royal Proclamation of 1763*, or under any treaty right made by agreement. The effect of this is that a right to, for example, equality cannot be used as an argument for derogating from Aboriginal and treaty rights. Therefore, on the face of it, the treaty as negotiated is afforded constitutional protection. This argument is not unproblematic. It is fair to say, however, that there is a *prima facie* argument arising from these provisions that any rights or powers emerging from the treaty are sheathed with constitutional protection.

While the NFA has the benefit of constitutional protection, it is stated in chapter 2, section 8 that it "does not alter the Constitution of Canada." This includes the division of powers between the federal and provincial government, the classification of Nisga'a people as Aboriginal people of Canada under the constitution, and the constitutional protections therein. Section 9, chapter 2 also ensures that "The *Canadian Charter of Rights and Freedoms* applies to Nisga'a Government in respect of all matters within its authority, bearing in mind the free and democratic nature of Nisga'a Government as set out in this Agreement." The application of the Charter to the treaty could be seen as a limitation of Nisga'a sovereignty. It circumscribes the actions of the NLG. It also can be viewed as the acceptance of the Charter by the Nisga'a, and the shared values of tolerance, equality, and freedoms that the document represents. This is a matter of perspective.

We are therefore left with some contradictory statements about the treaty's constitutional status. The NFA, and the rights and powers it contains, are constitutionally protected by section 35. It is also shielded from the operation of the Charter by section 25. In the treaty, however, the Charter is made to apply with the provision that its application must be done with the "free and democratic nature of the Nisga'a Government in mind." It is unclear whether this qualification will operate as a limitation on the NLG or an affirmation of it and its difference. If an equality right threatened the "free and democratic" Nisga'a government, could this be interpreted so as to apply Charter rights differently? The argument would be possible. The NFA also clearly states that the NFA does not alter the Constitution of Canada, yet it transfers power normally held by the provincial and federal governments to the Nisga'a Nation. The Agreement is therefore protected by the Constitution, excluded from the Charter's operation in the case where its interpretation derogates or abrogates an Aboriginal right, yet is also expressly bound by it. The NFA gets a quasi-constitutional status through the protection of Aboriginal rights in the Constitution, yet expressly does not change constitutional arrangements. Indeed, the NFA is a wonder of legal classification and paradox.

If we analyze these contradictions within a postcolonial framework, however, these incongruities can be understood differently. Homi Bhabha, borrowing from Jurgen Habermas, describes the postcolonial project as a desire to explore "widely scattered historical contingencies." He explains:

These contingencies are often the ground of historical necessity for elaborating empowering strategies of emancipation, staging other social antagonisms. To reconstitute the discourse of cultural difference demands not simply a change of cultural contents and symbols; a replacement within the same time-frame of representation is never adequate. It requires a radical revision of the social temporality in which emergent histories may be written, the rearticulation of the "sign" in which cultural identities may be inscribed. And contingency as a signifying time or counter-hegemonic strategies is not a celebration of "lack" or "excess"; or a self-perpetuating series of negative ontologies. Such "indeterminism" is the mark of the conflictual yet productive space in which the arbitrariness of the sign of cultural signification emerges within the regulated boundaries of social discourse.[30]

The constitutional status of the NFA is a fairly radical revision of the potential of the Canadian Constitution. The NFA transforms a document that articulates Canadian national sovereignty into a document that creates the space for the reemergence of the Nisga'a Nation. The constitution becomes a site of cultural contestation, a location where we see the "ability to shift the ground of knowledges, or to engage in the 'war of position,' [which] marks the establishment of new forms of meaning and strategies for identification."[31] Members of the Nisga'a Nation can now be Nisga'a and Canadian, with constitutional recognition of both.

An analysis of the balance of these provisions from a more practical strategic perspective suggests that there are different purposes that are being served by this ambiguous constitutional arrangement. The constitutional protection of the agreement ensures that, even with a change of the political winds, the NFA could not easily be shrugged aside. By, to phrase it crudely, "opting in" to the Charter, it becomes more difficult for the critics of national minority accommodation to accuse the NFA of allowing illiberalism to rule the day. The express declaration in the NFA that the treaty does not alter the Constitution may be a somewhat paradoxical, but possibly politically reassuring, confirmation that the NFA does not alter existing federal and provincial arrangements. This statement is possibly a reassurance that the Nisga'a political arrangements do not somehow supersede the existing Canadian political order. The applicability of the Charter to the exercise of Nisga'a authority is similarly reassuring. The Nisga'a have agreed that the exercise of their authority should be done within the principles enshrined in the Charter.

These uneasy and seemingly contradictory expressions reflect the difficult negotiation between the desire for "shared values" and a "shared identity" to bind together the political community,[32] and the need to recognize and protect cultural difference. While the Charter cannot be used to undermine the granting of power to the Nisga'a (s. 25), it should be applicable to the Nisga'a exercise of power. While the NFA does nothing to alter the existing constitutional arrangements in Canada, the Constitution protects the recognition of another level of *sui generis* government. The NFA (in legal terms) therefore simultaneously depends upon and challenges Canadian law. Indeed, this is the very heart of the postcolonial — moving beyond the shared colonial history into an uncertain postcolonial future.

Chapter 11 of the Agreement contains provisions on the nature and jurisdiction of the Nisga'a Lisims and Nisga'a Village governments. Section 1 states that "the Nisga'a Nation has the right to self-government, and the authority to make laws, as set out in this Agreement." Section 2 and 3 are provisions that recognize the jurisdiction of the NLG and NLV (Nisga'a Lisims Villages), and provide for their legal recognition. The Nisga'a therefore have a legally recognized village and national government with the capacity to enter into contracts, borrow or lend money, and sue or be sued. In contrast to life under the *Indian Act*, where Aboriginal groups were not afforded the legal status to engage independently in the economic sphere;[33] a legally recognized government with this capacity is a rather significant change. It represents a profound shift from a paternalistic system of administration, to a system that allows the Nisga'a people to participate in society as a collective entity, as well as individually, in all aspects of modern society.

Nisga'a governmental authority is, however, limited by three things: "The rights, powers, and privileges of the Nisga'a Nation, and of each Nisga'a Village, will be exercised in accordance with: a. [the] agreement, b. the Nisga'a Constitution, and c. Nisga'a Laws."[34] The power given to the Nisga'a is therefore not unfettered, and must ultimately be exercised within the parameters of the agreement. The limitation of the exercise of Nisga'a authority by the agreement is straightforward in principle, but also fundamentally problematic.

The Constitution also sets out the basic structure of Nisga'a government. Nisga'a government structure is itself a federal system. There is the Nisga'a Lisims Government (the central authority) and the Nisga'a Village Governments (the government structure of the four Villages — New Aiyansh, Laxgalts'ap, Gingolx, and Gitwinksihlkw). There are also Urban Locals in cities with a significant Nisga'a population, such as Prince Rupert, Terrace, and Vancouver. In addition to these levels of government, there is a Council of Elders composed of Simgigat, Sigidimhaanak, and respected Nisga'a elders whose role is to "advise Nisga'a Lisims Government on matters relating to the traditional values of the Nisga'a Nation." Simgigat are Nisga'a chiefs, and Sigidimhaanak are Nisga'a matriarchs.

The Nisga'a Lisims Government is constituted by a legislative house (Wilp Si'ayuukhl Nisga'a) and an executive branch. The Wilp Si'ayuukhl is made up of every individual who is an officer of the Nisga'a Lisims Government, the Chief Councillor of a Nisga'a Village Government, a Village Councillor of a Nisga'a village, and a representative from a Nisga'a Urban Local. The Council of Elders is not a regular part of the Wilp Si'ayuukhl, but can meet when a matter is referred to them by the Wilp Si'ayuukhl. The executive is composed of the president, the chairperson, the secretary-treasurer, the chairperson of the Council of Elders, and any other officer of the Nisga'a Lisims Government. Nisga'a Village Governments are composed of a Chief Councillor and a number of Village Councillors dependent upon how many residents live in the village.

There is a tension between First Nations' assertion of the right to self-government originating from before the European settlement of North America and the recognition (and limitation) of First Nation self-government rights through the treaty process. If First Nations rights are pre-existing rights, the treaty process, which places limitations on these inherent rights, seems contradictory to these principles. John Borrows explains the failure of the Canadian state to recognize Aboriginal sovereignty:

> Since Aboriginal people in British Columbia were not conquered and never agreed to relinquish their governmental rights, Aboriginal sovereignty should be placed on a footing equal or superior to Crown sovereignty. . . . The implications of the assertion of Crown sovereignty need to be more carefully scrutinized to assess the legality and justice of the non-consensual colonization of British Columbia. As it stands, the unequal treatment of Aboriginal and Crown sovereignty perpetuates historical injustices and fails to respect the distinctive legal systems of pre-existing Aboriginal societies in contemporary Canadian society.[35]

The NFA is a product of the overall unwillingness of the Canadian government and the courts to recognize Aboriginal self-government. The treaty, however, is not the product of "non-consensual colonization" but of a long process of negotiation. The Nisga'a, then, can be seen either as relinquishing their inherent (but as yet unrecognized) Aboriginal right to self-government, or as freely negotiating their way into the Canadian political community. It is difficult to exclusively defend either position. From the interviews I conducted, the truth seems to be somewhere in the middle. The members of the Nisga'a who were interviewed seemed to say that the treaty was indeed a recognition of their inherent rights to self-government, but was ultimately always going to have to be tempered by the political realities of the Canadian state. As Deanna Nyce stated, the "reality of treaties and negotiations is that people would not walk away with a hundred per cent — it would not happen."

For a population of approximately 2,500 Nisga'a who live on Nisga'a lands, and 3,500 who live outside Nisga'a land, it may seem that the multiple levels of government recognized by the constitution are unnecessary. In Nisga'a society, however, there was never a single central authority. Nisga'a governance has always been divided between the four clans or tribes — Laxsgiik (Eagle), Laxgibuu (Wolf), Gisk'aast (Killer Whale) and Ganada (Raven) — and their sub-crests. In addition, there were wilps (houses) and their leaders that were politically important. As it is stated in the Nisga'a Constitution, "In the same way that attachment to the land is central to the identity of every Nisga'a, the connection of families and communities to their traditional land has always been the basis of traditional authority within our nation."[36]

One supreme leader has never controlled all Nisga'a territory, and, not surprisingly, the Nisga'a have never had the notion of "radical title" held by one supreme ruler. If anything, it can be said that K'amligiihahlhat is the owner in "radical title" of the land. It is not therefore surprising that the Nisga'a did not create one unitary authority. Instead, the structure of Nisga'a government is more dispersed, as it has always been, with the Nisga'a Villages having legislative jurisdiction and authority as well.

Jurisdiction of the Nisga'a Lisims Government

If sovereignty means, as Deanna Nyce expressed, that "in my own house, I can make my own decisions . . . that I have a sense of place and responsibility for my sense of place,"[37] then the areas of governmental competency are the reflection of the areas in which the ability of the Nisga'a Nation to make decisions are important. In this section an overview of the areas of Nisga'a jurisdiction, both within and without the borders of their land, will be provided. Through this discussion I will demonstrate that the jurisdiction of the Nisga'a Nation provides the ability of the nation to internally facilitate their cultural values and rebuild a strong Nisga'a Nation that can emerge from the negative influences of colonial paternalism, and emerge as an equal participant in Canadian society. I will also demonstrate that the extra-territorial impacts foster the survival of the Nisga'a Nation in a multi-national Canadian state.

The general legislative authority of the Nisga'a Government is set out in Chapter 11. The Nisga'a Government has "principal authority . . . in respect of Nisga'a Government, Nisga'a citizenship, Nisga'a culture, Nisga'a language, Nisga'a Lands, and Nisga'a assets."[38] Nisga'a jurisdiction over government allows the Nisga'a to have prevailing authority over matters of governance such as elections and financial administration. This jurisdiction, however, is bounded by the provisions of the Agreement; elections, for example, must be held every five years. If there is a conflict with federal or provincial law, Nisga'a law will prevail. In this way, the Agreement provides the cornerstone of the relationship between the Nisga'a and the other Canadian governments. For example, if the federal government were to enact a law that specified certain procedures for all elections, and this law conflicted with a Nisga'a law, the Nisga'a law would prevail. The Nisga'a could not, however, enact a law that violated the election requirements in the Agreements. The Agreement, therefore, in relation to Nisga'a-Canadian relations is a "constitutional" document. If we put the issue of characterizing the relationship between the Agreement and the Canadian Constitution aside, the Agreement is the expression of the government-to-government relationship between the Nisga'a and the Canadian federal and provincial governments.

The Nisga'a also have primary jurisdiction over the definition of Nisga'a citizenship. The Agreement (section 5, chapter 2) contains a provision that defines the scope of the overall agreement, stating,

> The Nisga'a Nation represents and warrants to Canada and British Columbia that, in respect of the matters dealt with in this Agreement, it has the authority to enter, and it enters, into this Agreement on behalf of all persons who have any aboriginal rights, including aboriginal title, in Canada, or any claims to those rights, based on their identity as Nisga'a.

The governance jurisdiction therefore operates based on the assertion (and NLG recognition) of a Nisga'a identity. This is one of the issues that looms large in the current challenge to the Nisga'a Agreement being spearheaded by Chief Mountain, which will be discussed in the next chapter. Among the other grounds of the case, there is the basic challenge to the validity of the Agreement as representative, and binding upon, all people of Nisga'a identity. The

NLG has legislative jurisdiction to "make laws in respect of Nisga'a citizenship."[39] This jurisdiction allows the NLG to determine who has voting rights, for example. This jurisdiction is limited, though, by the proviso that Nisga'a citizenship and Canadian citizenship are not mutually exclusive. A citizen of the Nisga'a Nation is not denied any rights to Canadian citizenship.

Under the Nisga'a constitution, there is a broad but ambiguous definition of Nisga'a citizenship. The constitution states that "every Nisga'a participant who is a Canadian citizen or permanent resident of Canada is entitled to be a Nisga'a citizen."[40] Additionally, "a person who is not a Nisga'a participant and who is a Canadian citizen or a permanent resident of Canada may become a Nisga'a citizen if permitted by, and in accordance with Nisga'a law."[41] The definition in the constitution is limited by the enrollment provisions of the Agreement (chapter 20, section 1). These provisions state:

> An individual is eligible to be enrolled under this Agreement if that individual is:
> a. of Nisga'a ancestry and their mother was born into one of the Nisga'a tribes;
> b. a descendant of an individual described in subparagraphs 1 (a) or 1 (c);
> c. an adopted child of an individual described in subparagraphs 1 (a) or 1 (b); or
> d. an aboriginal individual who is married to someone described in subparagraphs 1 (a), (b), or (c) and has been adopted by one of the four Nisga'a tribes in accordance with Ayuukhl Nisga'a, that is, the individual has been accepted by a Nisga'a tribe, as a member of that tribe, in the presence of witnesses from the other Nisga'a tribes at a settlement or stone moving feast.

One cannot be enrolled under any other agreement or treaty. These criteria seem to exclude non-Aboriginal "participants" from being enrolled under the Agreement. The NLG website, however, states that a non-Aboriginal is

> entitled to become a Nisga'a citizen if that individual is not an Aboriginal individual, was a member of an Indian band before May 11, 2000, is a Canadian citizen or permanent resident of Canada, and is ordinarily resident on Nisga'a Lands. This individual cannot be enrolled under another land claims agreement. This person is or was married to a Nisga'a

participant and is adopted or taken in by one of the Nisga'a tribes in accordance with Ayuukhl Nisga'a.

Under this description a non-Aboriginal can become a Nisga'a through marriage and acceptance under Ayuukhl Nisga'a. Mere residency is not a sufficient criterion to become a Nisga'a citizen. This limitation can be seen as the failure of the NLG to recognize "universal suffrage." As Kymlicka has argued, however, "most liberal theorists accept without question that the world is, and will remain, composed of separate states, each of which is assumed to have the right to determine who can enter its borders and acquire citizenship."[42] If this is the case, then, "so far as liberal theorists accept the principle that citizenship can be restricted to the members of a particular group, the burden of proof lies on them to explain why they are not also committed to accepting group-differentiated rights within a state."[43] The Nisga'a are not therefore making any citizenship laws that are not familiar in any other nation.

This issue of entitlement illustrates a fundamental tension in the Nisga'a Agreement as a result of the argument for Aboriginal rights predicated upon a historical claim. If the basis, and normative legitimacy, for making agreements with First Nations is to redress the oppressive treatment of such groups, then the benefit of these agreements is intended to flow to the members of such groups. Citizenship, and therefore voting rights, should then be limited to the members of the First Nations group. But this was one of the most pressing criticisms of the Agreement raised in Chief Mountain's court case. He claimed that ethnically based citizenship goes against fundamental principles of democracy. As John Carpay has written, a fundamental principle of representation has been violated:

> Persons residing on Nisga'a land, who have been denied the right to vote, are still obligated to pay taxes to the Nisga'a "nation." This violates the principles of federalism, representative democracy, the rule of law, and democratic accountability; better known as the concept of "no taxation without representation."[44]

While the issue of ethnically exclusive citizenship is problematic within Western democratic terms, there is agreement among all nations that citizenship is not an automatic right. As Kymlicka explains, "group representation is a radical departure from the system of single-member geographically defined constituencies used in many Anglo-American democracies. And it does pose a challenge to our traditional notions of representation."[45] Limiting citizenship and rights, however, is nearly universally accepted within Western democracies. A person on a work visa in the UK has the right to work and pay taxes, for example, but no right to any social benefits such as Council Housing or even tax credits. Voting rights, in most cases,[46] are also denied. While in the UK, citizenship, for example, is not overtly culturally based, the introduction of a citizenship test does reflect that it is predicated broadly on acceptance of British cultural norms and values. The difference between the criteria for Nisga'a citizenship and UK citizenship is that Nisga'a citizenship is limited to one cultural group.

There is no easy way to resolve the deep tension between self-government based on ethnically determined citizenship and the fundamental values of individual equality and representation. In Canadian history, this tension has informed the most fundamental forging of the Canadian state. Indeed, the creation of the province of Manitoba through the *Manitoba Act* in 1870 was in response to the Métis resistance. This Act guaranteed the Métis title to their lands, as well as religious and language rights. These promises were never fulfilled, as white settlement was encouraged, ultimately forcing the Métis further west before their promised lands were secured. The *Manitoba Act* was, therefore, on its face a guarantee for the Métis, who had established a provisional government over the territory, which was ultimately defeated by the influx of European settlers. In more recent history, in the creation of Nunavut, an exclusively Inuit governmental structure was contemplated, but ultimately decided against. This decision was made because it was thought that, in the inhospitable climate of the Arctic, a public government was not a threat to Aboriginal representation.[47] Mass immigration of permanent residents to the Arctic is not all that likely.

Non-Nisga'a residents are not, however, omitted from consideration in the treaty. Chapter 11, section 19 states that the "Nisga'a Government will consult with individuals who are ordinarily resident within Nisga'a Lands and who are not Nisga'a citizens about Nisga'a Government decisions that directly and significantly affect them." Non-Nisga'a who are ordinarily resident within Nisga'a lands can also participate in Nisga'a public institutions if it relates to a matter that "may directly and significantly affect them."[48] They also are not denied from using the appeal or review procedures contained in the agreement. Non-Nisga'a can also be appointed as members of Nisga'a public institutions.

The effect of these provisions is to set up a layered citizenship, with all individuals within Nisga'a lands (who are legally entitled to the benefits of

Canadian political rights) enjoying the protection and benefits of the Canadian legal system, while citizens of the Nisga'a Nation are also entitled to enjoy the benefits and protection of the Nisga'a government. This approach to Indigenous rights has been called the "citizens plus" model.

If we refer back to chapter one, where Kymlicka's model of liberal accommodation was explored, liberalism may not be antithetical to cultural rights. The idea that a Nisga'a citizen (based on ethnicity) and a non-Nisga'a citizen have different political rights does, however, seem to stretch the limits of "liberal accommodation" Kymlicka ascribes to. He argues that the ability for one to live life according to one's values and beliefs is the justification for the accommodation of cultural practices:

> So we have two preconditions for the fulfillment of our essential interest in leading a life that is good. One is that we lead our lives from the inside, in accordance with our beliefs about what gives value to life; the other is that we be free to question those beliefs, to examine them in light of whatever information and examples and arguments our culture can provide. Individuals must therefore have the resources and liberties needed to live their lives in accordance with their beliefs about value, without being imprisoned or penalized for unorthodox religious or sexual practices etc.[49]

This model contemplates, as was argued, the inclusion of cultural rights such as religious practices and language rights, but cannot harmonize any practices that do not correspond with the liberal values of equality and autonomy. While the latter fundamental liberal value is not being threatened by the political arrangement created by the treaty, the former certainly is. A rights-based model, while still a matter of debate in relation to equality, is far more justifiable than a power-based model of Indigenous entitlement. The Nisga'a having the right to fish, based on the entitlement to continue their traditional practices, can be rationalized as restitution for past treatment. The Nisga'a have not only the right to fish, however, but the power to determine who should or should not fish within their territory. They are entitled to make laws about who can fish on their territory, without the democratic participation of all people who are resident on this territory. This inequality is inconsistent with a liberal idea of cultural accommodation. As Kymlicka writes,

Self-government rights, therefore, are the most complete case of differentiated citizenship, since they divide the people into separate "peoples," each with its own historic rights, territories, and powers of self-government; and each, therefore with its own political community. They may view their own political community as primary, and the value and authority of the larger federation as derivative.

. . .

Democratic multinational states which recognize self-government rights are, it appears, inherently unstable for this reason. At best they seem to be a *modus vivendi* between separate communities, with no intrinsic bond that would lead the members of one national group to make sacrifices for the other. Yet, as I noted earlier, liberal justice requires this sense of common purpose and mutual solidarity within the country.[50]

The NFA, as explained earlier, clearly creates a notion of differentiated citizenship. Through examining the specific jurisdictions of the Nisga'a Lisims Government, however, it becomes clear that Nisga'a self-government is indeed a *modus vivendi* between separate communities. It is still a "temporary accommodation of a disagreement between parties pending a permanent settlement."[51] From a postcolonial perspective, however, this is not an argument against such an arrangement, but a reflection of the realities of the post-colonial.

Social Jurisdiction of the Nisga'a Lisims Government

Earlier in this chapter, Carl Schmitt's "sovereign exception" was explained as potentially a way to gauge how meaningful Nisga'a sovereignty is within the NFA. The above section explored how Nisga'a jurisdiction over citizenship, despite liberal misgivings, allows them to define the membership of their nations, and who will benefit from it. Like Nisga'a land, in the case of the exception, they get the "power to exclude." Indeed, this is a fundamental aspect of sovereignty. Around the world, however, this power is often exercised with tanks rather than treaties. This section will explore NLG jurisdiction over social areas. In many of these areas, the NLG does not have exclusive paramountcy. They do, however, get meaningful control over areas of social life such as social services, marriage, health, education, adoption, and child custody. While the Nisga'a may not have paramountcy over these areas, the power that they have in the treaty gives them self-determination. It will be argued that it allows them to be the masters in their own house.

A postcolonial ethic is appropriate for self-government treaties in Canada, because it begins to challenge what self-government should mean. A Western understanding of sovereignty dictates national supremacy; a Foucauldian post-colonial understanding recognizes that sovereignty is not only about the power to sign international treaties. While in these areas the Nisga'a are not the final sovereign power in defining health care and education, the treaty gives them the power over the provision or delivery of these services. Indeed, it is possible that the evil of colonialism is not in the missionary intention to "elevate" Indigenous populations to the level of "Western" peoples, but in the misunderstanding that how one provides for aspects of "civilization" such as education and health care is necessarily different. Providing education for Aboriginal communities, for example, was done through removing children from their families to be educated in residential schools where they were subject to unthinkable abuse. Condemning this era of colonialism does not mean, however, that Aboriginal peoples should not have access to education. It does mean that the means by which this education is provided needs to be done in a different manner. Education does not threaten Nisga'a culture; colonial administration of education does.

Chapter 11 defines the NLG's jurisdiction over social areas. Section 78 defines Nisga'a Lisims Government jurisdiction over social services. The NLG is given jurisdiction to "make laws in respect of the provision of social services by Nisga'a Government to Nisga'a citizens, other than the licensing and regulation of facility-based services off Nisga'a Lands."[52] Unlike many of the powers discussed in this book, however, this is not an area where the Nisga'a have paramountcy. In the event of a conflict between a Nisga'a law and a federal or provincial law, the federal or provincial law prevails. Section 81 is one of the many provisions where negotiation is mandated if either party requests it.

The paramountcy of federal and provincial laws could be seen as a signal of continuing Nisga'a subordination to the Canadian state. The scope of the social services provision should, however, inform any judgement on the meaning of provincial and federal paramountcy. Social services in Canadian government terms include many meaningful benefits that Canadians enjoy, such as Employment Insurance, Child Tax Benefits, and Old Age Security Pension. The criticisms that Nisga'a citizens no longer enjoy the same benefits, or enjoy more benefits, as other Canadians would be warranted if the NLG had overriding jurisdiction in this area. As section 80 states, the NLG and the federal and provincial government will "attempt to reach agreement in respect of exchange of information, avoidance of double payments, and related matters." Nisga'a citizens here are again "citizens plus." They have access to Canadian social services, but may also benefit from Nisga'a social services.

The Nisga'a Lisims Government also has jurisdiction over the solemnization of marriages. In the Canadian federal system, the federal government has jurisdiction over marriage and divorce in section 91(26) of the Constitution. This includes the definition of marriage.[53] The provinces have jurisdiction over the solemnization of marriage in section 92(12) of the Constitution. This includes the recognition of those able to perform marriages, and licensing and registration requirements.[54] Chapter 11, section 75–77, defines NLG jurisdiction in regards to the solemnization of marriages. These provisions allow the NLG to make laws in respect to the solemnization of marriages, including the ability to authorize individuals to perform legal marriages. These people will, under the treaty, be duly authorized to solemnize marriages under British Columbia and Nisga'a law, enjoying "all the associated rights, duties and responsibilities of a marriage commissioner under the provincial *Marriage Act*."

To illustrate the significance of the shared jurisdiction, some explanation of the regulation of the solemnization of marriage is necessary. Under the B.C. *Marriage Act*, to become authorized to conduct marriages one must be registered as a religious representative, or as a marriage commissioner (in civil marriages). To become an authorized religious representative, an application must be made to the chief executive officer under the *Vital Statistics Act*.[55] The person must, among other things, be a resident of British Columbia who is properly ordained as part of a recognized religion (section 3). Marriage commissioners are appointed by the minister (section 32).

While in the event of a conflict between Nisga'a laws and provincial and federal laws the latter will prevail, the authority of the Nisga'a Lisims Government to make laws in relation to the solemnization of marriages illustrates an important aspect of Nisga'a self-determination. While each village in the Nass Valley has its own church, with its own officials who are currently able to solemnize marriages, this provision gives the NLG the ability to make laws allowing, for example, respected elders in the community who would have traditionally provided such services to the community to become able to perform marriages without being appointed through the provincial system. If one considers how remote the Nass Valley is, and the fact that many of the respected elders still live in very traditional ways, this could be an important tool for symbolically reauthorizing Nisga'a cultural values through greater official participation in important ceremonies. This is not to say that before these individuals were legally empowered to preside over marriages that they did not play an important role in marriages; this role was, however, placed in a subordinate position to the defining authority of the provincial government. If the NLG can allow for elders and other respected Nisga'a to be legally recognized to solemnize marriages, it signals that the Nisga'a Nation is a valid and recognized entity within the Canadian state. It signals that the Nisga'a Nation can exercise power within the state, rather than being subject exclusively to the provincial exercise of power.

The final social area that will be examined where the NLG has jurisdiction is in education. The NLG may make laws for both the provision of preschool to grade twelve education (s. 100–102), as well as for the provision of post-secondary education. This includes the certification of teachers, and the teaching of Nisga'a language and culture. In the event of a conflict, Nisga'a law will prevail. These provisions, however, include the requirement in both areas that the education provided be comparable to the education provided in other schools in British Columbia. Section 100, for example, provides that in relation to pre-school to grade 12, the laws include provisions for "curriculum, examination, and other standards that permit transfers of students between school systems at a similar level of achievement and permit admission of students to the provincial post-secondary education systems." Section 102 also provides that the NLG and the provincial government, upon request of either party, will negotiate to reach agreement in relation to post-secondary education "persons other than Nisga'a citizens residing within Nisga'a Lands" and "Nisga'a citizens residing off Nisga'a Lands."[56]

Nisga'a jurisdiction over education plays a fundamental role in the strength of the Nisga'a Nation. As Pat Moores (the non-Nisga'a superintendent of the school district) observed, the introduction of programs such as Nisga'a language teaching has had a positive effect. He commented that "children achieve better if they have an identity." As the 2004-2005 School District Review reported, school district 92 (Nisga'a) is unique in that it is more homogenous than other school districts, with ninety per cent of students being Aboriginal as compared to five per cent provincially. This report identified some of the strengths of the school district as "pride in the Nisga'a culture," a "high percentage of qualified Nisga'a teachers and staff," a "strong 'web of support' reflected in community connections with government, schools, staff, Elders and families," and "holistic approach towards student education from Head Start to adult education."[57]

In relation to post-secondary education, Nisga'a laws will also prevail in the event of a conflict. Provisions are made, however, that require the laws

> will include standards comparable to provincial standards in respect of: a. institutional organizational structure and accountability; b. admission standards and policies; c. instructors' qualifications and certification; d. curriculum standards sufficient to permit transfers of students between provincial post-secondary institutions; and e. requirements for degrees, diplomas, or certificates.

The NLG may make laws in relation to establishing post-secondary institutions, determining the curriculum, and accrediting teachers; however, the provision made must allow students in Nisga'a institutions to meet requirements comparable to other post-secondary institutions.

While the treaty gave the NLG powers in relation to post-secondary education, the Nisga'a Tribal Council had earlier established a Nisga'a post-secondary institution in 1993. Wilp Wilxo'oskwhl Nisga'a (WWN: Nisga'a House of Wisdom) was created "to provide quality post-secondary education and training to people within the Nisga'a community, and to ensure the survival of Nisga'a language and culture.'"[58] In 1999, when this institution graduated four students with bachelor's degrees, "it was the first time in Canada that First Nations students earned degrees in their own, Aboriginal communities."[59] The WWN is a non-profit organization affiliated with the University of Northern British Columbia, Northwest Community College, and Royal Roads University for the delivery and accreditation of its courses and programs. It is not, per se, a degree-granting institution, but its importance is that members of the Nisga'a Nation can take courses in the Nass Valley rather than having to move to Prince George or elsewhere. The WWN has Nisga'a language and culture courses, as well as a range of other courses taught in other Canadian institutions. Deanna Nyce, the CEO of WWN, explained the importance of this institution in its ability to offer training for Nisga'a people without them having to move away from the Nass Valley. Indeed, some of the graduates of the school are now working in the Nass Valley in key roles that once had to be filled by non-Nisga'a. She also explained that the Nisga'a language and culture courses were playing a key role in reinvigorating Nisga'a culture. In important ceremonies such as feasts, Nisga'a language and cultural literacy were acting as a barrier for Nisga'a participation. The WWN, therefore, offers a way that Nisga'a who have not been taught Nisga'a language and cultural practices can become full participants in their own culture.

One of the dominant fears about self-government and self-determination of national minorities is that it would inevitably lead to the splintering of the national political community and the weakening of national ties. Nisga'a jurisdiction over social services, marriage, and education, however, provides not only a mechanism for the strengthening of the Nisga'a Nation, but also for more Nisga'a participation in the Canadian political community. In a speech about the mission of the WWN, Sim'oogit Bayt Neekhl (Jacob McKay) said,

> Only by learning to share did the Nisga'a people flourish in our rugged and isolated corner of British Columbia. Today, we are forging full partnerships with other educational institutions in order to provide top quality, culturally appropriate post secondary education to everyone who lives here in the Nass River Valley. Increasingly, we welcome students from other parts of the world as well.[60]

This is not a project of the Nisga'a Nation moving away from the Canadian political community, but one of rebuilding their capacity to better participate in it to the betterment of all Canadians.

Conclusion

The Nisga'a have not achieved what would ordinarily be recognized in international politics as "sovereignty" with the signing of the Nisga'a Final Agreement. They have, however, achieved a treaty that gives them a voice within the Canadian state. If we refer back to the discussion of sovereignty earlier in this chapter, this may be an entirely appropriate version of sovereignty for First Nations. As Burch has argued, "one might better see (conceive) that sovereignty is neither a condition nor a characteristic. Rather, sovereignty is a social practice. Sovereignty is made, maintained and exercised."[61] The question becomes whether the NFA and its implementation is the exercise of such a version of sovereignty. If we apply the "sovereign exception" to the Nisga'a Final Agreement, wherever the Nisga'a Lisims Government has paramountcy they do exercise sovereignty. Indeed, they exercise sovereignty over one key aspect of nationhood — membership. Over areas where there is shared jurisdiction, such as social services, it would be disingenuous to criticize the treaty for not giving the NLG paramountcy, as independence in these areas would remove members of the Nisga'a Nation from the benefits enjoyed by all Canadians such as employment insurance and the Canada pension. The answer to the question of whether the NFA makes the Nisga'a sovereign is therefore yes — if one imagines a postcolonial notion of sovereignty. Indeed, if the NFA can transform the Canadian constitution into a site for "the establishment of new forms of meaning," it is also a site that changes the signification of sovereignty. As Bhabha writes, cultural difference

> changes the position of enunciation and the relation of address within it; not only what is said but where it is said; not simply the logic of articulation but the topos of enunciation. The aim of cultural difference is to rearticulate the sum of knowledge from the perspective of the signifying position of the minority that resists totalization — the repetition that will not return as the same, the minus-in-origin that results in political and discursive strategies where adding *to* does not add up but serves to disturb the calculation of power and knowledge, producing other spaces of subaltern signification.[62]

If "nations, like narratives, lose their origins in the myths of time and only fully realize their horizons in the mind's eye,"[63] is it hard to imagine that the epistemological foundation of the nation cannot be the subject to subaltern revision. The intervention of the NFA into Canadian constitutionalism does not add to Canadian sovereignty, but it does revise it.

○

CHAPTER FIVE

The Courts

Introduction

The previous three chapters have explored how the Nisga'a Final Agreement[1] mediates between Aboriginal rights and Aboriginal powers to reflect a model of Nisga'a self-government that expresses the Nisga'a Nation's aspirations as a viable contemporary self-determining entity within Canada. In chapter four, it was argued that the NFA reflects a postcolonial sovereignty that allows internal self-determination on some matters, and creates a framework for external negotiation in relation to others. In this chapter, I argue that the court challenges of the NFA demonstrate the anxiety that these self-determination powers are creating — both from without and within the Nisga'a Nation.

In this chapter, I argue that two court challenges questioning the constitutional validity of the NFA demonstrate that the treaty has become sheathed with the constitutional protection of state sovereignty afforded to the Canadian government. While during negotiations the Nisga'a Nation and the provincial and federal governments were clearly on opposite sides of the table, after the treaty they find themselves all defending its validity.

These cases demonstrate that sovereignty is not merely the effect of an original authority that validates a sovereign's power; rather, it is the exercise of power that instantiates sovereignty. In other words, sovereignty is not something a sovereign owns or inherits, it is the effect of practicing sovereignty. The NFA recognizes the power of the Nisga'a to make laws. Through exercising this power, the Nisga'a Nation and its government are becoming sovereign. According to the *Campbell*[2] and the *Chief Mountain*[3] decisions, this sovereignty is becoming tied to the sovereignty of Canada. To describe this process in different terms, the Nisga'a have come full circle from having their right to self-determination slowly undermined by the colonial exercise of power to reclaiming their right to self-determination by exercising their authority under the treaty. The effect of this recognition is the revision of

Canadian sovereignty as the product of both Aboriginal and Canadian law, rather than a unitary and exclusively liberal sovereignty.

I am not arguing that the treaty has effectively resolved the issues that have been endemic since Western settlement. What I am arguing is that the powers provided to the Nisga'a Nation in the NFA provide a structure that can allow the beginning of a process of decolonization. I believe it is a danger to take a short view of reconciliation. If we consider that First Nations have been subjected to devastating colonial policies in Canada for over two centuries, it is hardly surprising that developing a truly postcolonial model of governance will take more than a few decades.

The Campbell Case

The negotiation of the NFA was a highly charged political matter. Opposition to the treaty was expressed by citizens groups such as the BC F.I.R.E (BC Foundation for Individual Equality), and joined by opposition party politicians. The government in power during the negotiations was the New Democratic Party, which lies to the left on the Canadian political spectrum. While they backed the treaty negotiation, the official opposition used the negotiation of the treaty as a political platform. Liberal leader Gordon Campbell, the leader of the official opposition, was quoted in the Vancouver *Sun* on April 8, 1998, as saying, "Indeed, the only thing worse than no treaties are [sic] seriously flawed treaties imposed against the wishes of British Columbians."[4] As Tom Molloy explains, the public political resistance to the treaty incited response from the Nisga'a negotiators:

> [I]n a pair of articles published in the Vancouver *Sun* in early April, Liberal leader Gordon Campbell had suggested that one of the first steps in treaty making should be a mandate that was acceptable to the majority of British Columbians. This mandate, of course, could only come from a province-wide referendum. Certainty and equality, he insisted, could only be attained through extinguishment and the exclusion of "third order of government" arrangements. Not surprisingly, this did not go down well at the negotiating table, particularly among the Nisga'a. Joe Gosnell was quoted in the April 12 issue of the Vancouver *Province*: "It is not for the government to extinguish who we are as people, because they didn't place us on this land. We prefer to sit across the table and discuss how to reconcile our rights as Nisga'a and your rights as Canadians."[5]

This statement reflects the political battleground on which the treaty was negotiated. The political opposition framed the starting point of negotiation as the definition of acceptable norms by popular vote of the (non-Aboriginal) majority. The Nisga'a negotiators insisted that nothing less than nation-to-nation negotiation was acceptable. This reflects the Nisga'a insistence on a negotiation mandate authorized not by the dominant majority but based on negotiation between the authority of the Canadian political mandate and the Nisga'a Nation's independent legitimacy.

Gordon Campbell, Michael G. deJong, and Geoffrey Plant, who were all members of the official opposition at the time, eventually took their political platform into the judicial arena. In 2000, a case was launched challenging the constitutionality of the Nisga'a Final Agreement. The plaintiffs sought "an order declaring that the Nisga'a Treaty recently concluded between Canada, British Columbia and the Nisga'a Nation is in part inconsistent with the Constitution of Canada and therefore in part of no force and effect."[6] At the heart of the challenge was the claim that any area where the Nisga'a Lisims Government laws were paramount over provincial or federal law was inconsistent with the Canadian Constitution. This case was therefore not challenging the aspects of the treaty that defined Aboriginal rights, only the areas where there was recognition of Aboriginal powers.

Justice L. P. Williamson of the British Columbia Supreme Court summarized the plaintiffs' arguments as follows:

> In short, they say that the Treaty violates the Constitution because parts of it purport to bestow upon the governing body of the Nisga'a Nation legislative jurisdiction inconsistent with the exhaustive division of powers granted to Parliament and the Legislative Assemblies of the Provinces by Sections 91 and 92 of the *Constitution Act, 1867*. Second, they submit the legislative powers set out in the treaty interfere with the concept of royal assent. Finally, they argue that by granting legislative power to citizens of the Nisga'a Nation, non-Nisga'a Canadian citizens who reside in or have other interests in the territory subject to Nisga'a government are denied rights guaranteed to them by Section 3 of the *Canadian Charter of Rights and Freedoms*.[7]

Section 3 guarantees voting rights.

The first claim was premised upon the understanding of the Canadian Constitution and its enumeration of federal and provincial powers in section 91 and 92 as an exclusive, exhaustive, and inviolable list of the sovereign powers of Canadian government. An acceptance of this interpretation of the Constitution would exclude any area of Nisga'a jurisdiction that was carved out of these powers. The second argument is that Nisga'a lawmaking powers are contrary to s. 55 of the *Constitution Act, 1867*. In essence, the treaty enables the Nisga'a Lisims Government to make laws that will not be given royal assent as required by section 55; while the treaty itself was given assent by both the BC Legislature and Parliament, it enables the creation of laws that will not.[8] The third ground was that the Agreement violated the constitutional right of all Canadians to democratically participate in elections of Canadian law-making bodies. This third argument, however, was predicated on the first argument. Laws made under the powers in the NFA would only fall afoul of this provision if the court was to find that the Canadian Constitution was an exclusive inventory of valid law-making power in Canada. Section 3 only protects a Canadian citizen's right to vote in elections for the members of the House of Commons and the legislative assembly of one's province of residence. If the NLG is (unconstitutionally) exercising provincial or federal legislative functions, then non-Nisga'a citizens being denied the vote would potentially infringe this right.

The BC Supreme Court rejected the argument that the Canadian constitution exhaustively enumerates legitimate law-making powers. Justice Williamson's analysis of the Canadian Constitution instead reflects a fluid notion of Canadian sovereignty and federalism. He did not agree that the enumerated division of powers is the exclusive and exhaustive enunciation of Canadian governmental jurisdiction. The plaintiffs relied upon the characterization of the division of powers enunciated in the 1912 case of *A.G. Ontario* v. *A.G. Canada*.[9] In this case, it was stated:

> Now, there can be no doubt that under this organic instrument the powers distributed between the Dominion on the one hand and the provinces on the other hand cover the whole area of self-government within the whole area of Canada.[10]

If this was indeed the case, and the Constitution is an exhaustive enunciation of legislative power in Canada, any areas of Nisga'a law-making power would be wholly unconstitutional.

Mr. Justice Williamson instead drew on more recent cases on Canadian cultural diversity. He drew from the Quebec *Secession Reference*[11] where the purpose of the Canadian Constitution was interpreted within its historical terms of reference. In that case, the Canadian constitution was described as "the legal recognition of the diversity that existed among the initial members of Confederation, and manifested a concern to accommodate that diversity within a single nation. Federalism was the political mechanism by which diversity could be reconciled with unity."[12] Drawing also on the *Guerin* case, Justice Williamson instead characterizes the Canadian Constitution as an "internal" declaration of the legislative competencies of the provincial and federal government. As former Chief Justice Dickson explained in *Mitchell*, "from the aboriginal perspective, any federal-provincial divisions that the Crown has imposed on itself are internal to itself and do not alter the basic structure of Sovereign-Indian relations."[13] Aboriginal self-government therefore survived "as one of the unwritten 'underlying values' of the Constitution outside of the powers distributed to Parliament and the legislatures in 1867. The federal-provincial division of powers in 1867 was aimed at a different issue and was a division 'internal' to the Crown."[14]

If we recall the development of Aboriginal rights jurisprudence in Canada, this statement is truly revolutionary. In the *Van der Peet*[15] case, the Supreme Court expressed that the purpose of section 35, which protects Aboriginal and treaty rights, is "the reconciliation of the pre-existence of distinctive aboriginal societies with the assertion of Crown sovereignty. Courts adjudicating aboriginal rights claims must, therefore, be sensitive to the aboriginal perspective, but they must also be aware that aboriginal rights exist within the general legal system of Canada."[16] This statement has been taken by academics such as Peter Fitzpatrick to express the "unchallengeable" sovereignty that he argues continues to defeat any meaningful claim for Aboriginal rights.[17] Recognizing that Aboriginal self-government survived "outside" the Canadian constitutional order as an "underlying value" seems to be in direct opposition to a notion of Aboriginal rights as being limited by the federal system. Indeed, Justice Williamson explains that "the assertion of Crown sovereignty and the ability of the Crown to legislate in relation to lands held by Aboriginal groups does not lead to the conclusion that powers of self-government held by those Aboriginal groups were eliminated."[18]

The fundamental assumption on which the plaintiffs' argument was premised — that the assertion of Canadian sovereignty extinguished any claim for First Nation self-government — was rejected. As Justice Williamson wrote, "The heart of this argument is that any right to such self-government or legislative power was extinguished at the time of Confederation. Thus, the plaintiffs distinguish aboriginal title and other aboriginal rights, such as the right to hunt or to fish, from the right to govern one's own affairs."[19] Therefore, while the recognition of Aboriginal rights can be reconciled with the Canadian Constitution, any legislative jurisdiction recognized by the treaty is invalid and unconstitutional. In the judgement, this argument was quickly undermined when Mr. Justice Williamson summarized Nisga'a-Canadian relationship as demonstrating "that the Nisga'a never ceded their rights or lands to the Crown. The Treaty which is now the subject of this litigation marks the first occasion upon which the Nisga'a have agreed to any specified impairment of those rights."[20] Second, Justice Williamson concluded from Nisga'a history that "the fact that the Crown in right of Canada and the Crown in right of British Columbia have entered into these negotiations, and concluded an Agreement, illustrates that the Crown accepts the Nisga'a Nation has the authority to bargain with the State and possesses rights which are negotiable."[21] This is a much-changed assumption of First Nation history than earlier jurisprudence, and from these truths come a much different analysis.

This interpretation of Aboriginal sovereignty, and its positioning in relation to the Constitution of Canada, represents a fundamental revision of a notion of Canadian sovereignty. This argument is reflected in John Ralston Saul's recent book, *A Fair Country: Telling Truths About Canada,*[22] in which he argues that Canada is a Métis[23] nation. He argues that Canada has always been instantiated by settler's relations to First Nations. In the words of one reviewer, Saul argues that Canada has "been heavily influenced and shaped by aboriginal ideas: egalitarianism, a proper balance between individual and group, and a penchant for negotiation over violence are all aboriginal values that Canada absorbed."[24] Canada's peculiar rights culture is therefore a product of Aboriginal influence on the Canadian political community. The argument that First Nations are a legitimate source of authority is not only recognized in the context of treaty negotiations by the courts, but is also being accepted within a broader discursive realm. To reiterate Tuitt's sentiments in "Postcolonial Theory at the Moment of Judgment," we can frame the implications of this acceptance in a fairly radical way:

> Can legal texts as well as literary texts ever reach a fully achieved state? Can legal texts accommodate the practice of naming? It has already been said that the relationship between the colonial source text and the postcolonial re-writing is in a sense institutionalized in law. The question of whether that institutional practice can be disturbed is closely

tied to the question of whether the legal institution can accommodate naming as a practice that might allow a fully achieved postcolonial legal text to be seized by the postcolonial proper. The question can be put another way: can the colonial legal source be confused, obscured with its many other competing sources, such that we can talk not of a singular source of origin but several or at least more than one. It is to be recalled that this question is not relevant to the formal authority of a legal text or its value as precedent since a postcolonial legal re-writing can overrule or invalidate its colonial source and take away the power of the colonial source to deal "pain and death."[25]

Indeed, it seems that the characterization of Canadian sovereignty, as expressed in the Canadian Constitution, is only one source of sovereign power and cultural authority.

The second argument the plaintiffs made in the *Campbell* case was the Nisga'a law-making authority was unconstitutional because it circumvented the constitutional requirement for royal assent. Section 55 of the Canadian Constitution requires laws passed by the Houses of Parliament to be granted royal assent by the Queen's representative in Canada (the Governor General). The plaintiffs argued that any laws made under the authority if the NFA would be unconstitutional because this procedural requirement is lacking. Relying on the case *re The Initiative and Referendum Act*,[26] the plaintiffs argued that it is unconstitutional for a Canadian body of government to "create and endow with its own capacity a new legislative power not created by the *British North America Act* to which it owes it own existence."[27] In that case, the Manitoba government tried to pass an act that would allow for a process by which, if a referendum was passed on a matter, the matter would automatically become law without having to go through the ordinary law-making procedures, including royal assent. Justice Williamson found that the Nisga'a Treaty was not analogous to the *Manitoba Referendum Act* for two reasons. First, he stated that the NFA is not a "'profound constitutional upheaval' . . . the powers granted to the Nisga'a Nation in the Treaty are limited and are within those contemplated by Section 35 of the *Constitution Act, 1982*."[28] Second, section 55 "does not on its wording apply to other law-making bodies."[29]

The first reason given is that the powers granted to the Nisga'a Nation in the NFA do not profoundly affect the powers in the Canadian Constitution, because they are found within it. Section 35, which enshrines "existing aboriginal and treaty rights," includes Nisga'a self-government, so it should not be seen as a constitutional upheaval but rather an ordinary constitutional matter. It is not difficult to recognize how profoundly the judicial discourse on Aboriginal self-government has shifted, considering the arguments that were being made and accepted in the Canadian courts for the majority of the twentieth century. Justice McEachern in *Delgamuukw* described Aboriginal peoples' "laws and customs [as] not sufficiently certain to permit a finding that they or their ancestors governed the territory according to aboriginal laws even though some Indians may well have chosen to follow local customs when it was convenient to do so."[30] In *Delgamuukw*, Aboriginal peoples never had laws; in *Campbell*, Aboriginal laws are recognized and protected. Through this reasoning, we see the Canadian Constitution interpreted not as an expression of the unlimited sovereign power of the government, but as a document prescribing the limitations on Canadian governance; these same limitations, however, do not apply to the NLG.

The interpretation of the constitution as a document limiting the government's law-making power is explicitly adopted. Justice Williamson is of the view that section 55 only applies to the federal House of Commons and provincial legislatures. Laws made by the Nisga'a Lisims Government do not require royal assent pursuant to section 55. This logic relies on the court's finding that the recognition of First Nation government is an "underlying value" of the Canadian Constitution, but also outside the limited confines of its enumeration of powers. In an extraordinarily postcolonial way, the Nisga'a are the "other" that can be both marginal, and central — the outside brought within. They are authorized by the Canadian Constitutional order, yet not limited by it.

The third argument made by the plaintiffs was that Nisga'a law-making power violates section 3 of the *Canadian Charter of Rights and Freedoms* by depriving Canadian citizens from the right to vote for their political representatives. This argument is premised on the limitation of political rights in the Nass Valley to those who qualify under the treaty. Full political rights are granted only to people who qualify to be members of the Nisga'a Nation through the criteria described in chapter four. Justice Williamson, citing the *Secession reference*, quoted the following passage that describes the rights enshrined in section 3: "Historically, this Court has interpreted democracy to mean the process of representative and responsible government and the right of citizens to participate in the political process as voters and as candidates."[31] Under the Nisga'a Final Agreement, full democratic participation is limited to Nisga'a citizens. The argument that Nisga'a law-making power is unconstitutional is premised on the situation whereby an individual may live in the Nass Valley but be denied the right to participate in the government because they are not Nisga'a citizens, and therefore not allowed full political citizenship. This differentiated citizenship has been compared to apartheid.[32]

The argument that Nisga'a law-making powers violate section 3 of the Charter is dismissed, however, based on several alternative arguments. First, Justice Williamson dismissed the claim because the assertion that Nisga'a law-making power violates section 3 is predicated on the finding that the Nisga'a government is exercising powers reserved for the federal or provincial government under section 91 and 92 of the Constitution. If the Nisga'a are exercising federal and provincial jurisdiction, then it would be the case that all the citizens of Canada are being deprived of their political right to vote and run in the elections of the body that exercises such powers. As he decided that section 91 and 92 are not exhaustive and exclusive articulations of Canadian legislative powers, this argument is "seriously undermined" and therefore dismissed.[33]

In the alternative, Justice Williamson posits that section 25 of the Constitution would answer the challenge. Even if the Nisga'a law-making powers were in violation of section 3, he asserts that section 25 ensures that Charter rights shall not "abrogate or derogate from any aboriginal, treaty or other rights or freedoms that pertain to the aboriginal peoples of Canada." He initially points out that "one must keep in mind that the communal nature of aboriginal rights is on the face of it at odds with the European/North American concept of individual rights articulated in the Charter."[34] Additionally, he cited Supreme Court of Canada jurisprudence that encourages "where there is ambiguity, constitutional or statutory provisions are to be given a large and liberal interpretation in favour of aboriginal peoples."[35]

On a more basic level of participatory democracy, Justice Williamson echoed the argument that Kymlicka makes about the accepted right for non-citizens to be denied voting rights. Williamson pointed out that there are many circumstances where provincial residency requirements or other restrictions may validly limit political participation. If within the Canadian state voting rights are limited by things such as residency requirements, it is therefore not by extension a violation for the Nisga'a to have requirements that exclude individuals. The difference between the type of criteria that limits enfranchisement for provincial elections, however, is cultural membership rather than mere residency. The difference in quality between these criteria for voting rights is not mentioned in Justice Williamson's reasoning.

Williamson, therefore, concluded not only that the Nisga'a Final Agreement and its paramount law-making powers are not unconstitutional, but are protected by the Constitution of Canada. The NFA is therefore characterized as a document that creates the substantive content of section 35 which guarantees Aboriginal and treaty rights:

> I have concluded that after the assertion of sovereignty by the British Crown, and continuing to and after the time of Confederation, although the right of aboriginal people to govern themselves was diminished, it was not extinguished. Any aboriginal right to self-government could be extinguished after Confederation and before 1982 by federal legislation which plainly expressed that intention, or it could be replaced or modified by the negotiation of a treaty. Post-1982, such rights cannot be extinguished, but they may be defined (given content) in a treaty. The Nisga'a Final Agreement does the latter expressly.[36]
>
> . . .
>
> Section 35 of the *Constitution Act, 1982*, then, constitutionally guarantees, among other things, the limited form of self-government which remained with the Nisga'a after the assertion of sovereignty. The Nisga'a Final Agreement and the settlement legislation give that limited right definition and content. Any decision or action which results from the exercise of this now-entrenched treaty right is subject to being infringed upon by Parliament and the legislative assembly. This is because the Supreme Court of Canada has determined that both aboriginal and treaty rights guaranteed by s. 35 may be impaired if such interference can be justified and is consistent with the honour of the Crown.[37]

This case, therefore, demonstrates that there are two very different ways of characterizing First Nation self-government. The first, articulated by the plaintiffs, is that it is a challenge to Canadian sovereignty. The second, asserted by the Nisga'a Nation, is that self-government is the instantiation of an expression of Canadian sovereignty as articulated through the Canadian Constitution. In the *Campbell* case, Justice Williamson characterized the NFA as the elaboration and definition of fundamental principles of the Canadian constitutional order. Indeed, it seems that the NFA may give us clues about how to answer the question of what "might allow a fully achieved postcolonial legal text to be seized by the postcolonial proper?" In this case, we see the recognition of "other competing sources" of sovereignty, "such that we can talk not of a singular source of origin."[38]

The *Campbell* decision demonstrates an understanding of sovereignty that moves beyond a liberal accommodation model into a postcolonial dynamic of power-sharing. I have argued that this power-sharing model is fundamentally premised on a distinction between Aboriginal rights and Aboriginal power. Aboriginal rights have been traditionally defined by the dominant legal system. Aboriginal power can be described as the mechanisms that allow for Aboriginal peoples to define their own social, cultural, and economic priorities. Aboriginal rights discourse, therefore, constructs Aboriginal peoples as historical curiosities frozen in the time of European "discovery." Instantiations of Aboriginal power, such as in the NFA, on the other hand, recognize First Nations power to self-determine as a contemporary people. The *Campbell* case is that remarkable moment when, as Tuitt has described, "recognition of the postcolonial text as equal at least in its right, its 'power' to determine meanings in the colonial text is expunged."[39] Instead, from the vague, amorphous guarantee of Aboriginal rights enunciated in *Delgamuukw*, we begin to see the actual materiality of Aboriginal sovereignty emerge.

The Chief Mountain Case

The story does not end with the British Columbia Supreme Court's decision in the *Campbell* case. An appeal was launched. On June 5, 2001, Gordon Campbell was sworn in as Premier of British Columbia after the Liberal party was elected with the largest majority in British Columbia's history. In 2001, the appeal was dropped. As the newly appointed Attorney General of British Columbia, Geoffrey Plant is reported as saying, "Now that we're in government, it's not possible to sue ourselves."[40] In the same article, it was reported that "Plant said the Liberals feel it's time to recognize that the former government made commitments to the Nisga'a, and to support those commitments."[41]

The Liberal party did, however, conduct a referendum on Aboriginal treaties in 2002. The outcome was overwhelmingly in favour of the eight principles proposed in the referendum:

1. Private property should not be expropriated for treaty settlements. (Yes/No)

2. The terms and conditions of leases and licenses should be respected; fair compensation for unavoidable disruption of commercial interests should be ensured. (Yes/No)

3. Hunting, fishing and recreational opportunities on Crown land should be ensured for all British Columbians. (Yes/No)

4. Parks and protected areas should be maintained for the use and benefit of all British Columbians. (Yes/No)

5. Province-wide standards of resource management and environmental protection should continue to apply. (Yes/No)

6. Aboriginal self-government should have the characteristics of local government, with powers delegated from Canada and British Columbia. (Yes/No)

7. Treaties should include mechanisms for harmonizing land use planning between Aboriginal governments and neighbouring local governments. (Yes/No)

8. The existing tax exemptions for Aboriginal people should be phased out. (Yes/No)

A Yes vote means the government will be bound to adopt the principle in treaty negotiations.

A No vote means the government will not be bound to adopt the principle to guide its participation in treaty negotiations.[42]

This referendum was criticized for the implications of the principles proposed. These questions reflected assumptions about the treaty process that were plainly inflammatory. Question one, for example, seemed to suggest that treaty settlements threatened privately owned land by the possibility of expropriation of existing private property rights. Question two implied that treaties will create "unavoidable" disruptions to existing commercial arrangements. Question 3 implied that Aboriginal treaties will exclude non-Aboriginal British Columbians from hunting, fishing, and other recreational activities on Crown land. Question 4 presumed that treaties threaten the access of British Columbians to parks, and so on.

Unsurprisingly, the referendum sparked outrage in British Columbia. As one article reported,

the referendum was controversial from the outset. Critics, including native and church leaders, called the plebiscite "stupid," "immoral," "amateurish," and "racist." By the May 15 deadline, only about one third of the mail-in ballots were returned. Many ballots were burned. Others were turned into paper airplanes, cut into snowflakes, even toilet paper.[43]

In the same article, Angus Reid, a veteran pollster, called the referendum "one of the most amateurish, one-sided attempts to gauge the public will that I have seen in my professional career."[44]

Thus, while the legal challenge was ended, the political discourse continued. Gordon Campbell and his fellow MLAs were not the only people discontented with the treaty, however, and another legal challenge was launched even before the decision was rendered in the *Campbell* case. This claim was put forth by Chief Mountain, an ancestral Nisga'a Chief. Chief Mountain claims that the Nisga'a Final Agreement is unconstitutional under section 52, which states that "the Constitution of Canada is the supreme law of Canada, and any law that is inconsistent with the provisions of the Constitution is, to the extent of the inconsistency, of no force or effect." More specifically, he charged that the law-making authority provided for in the NFA was contrary to the division of powers in the Constitution. Finally he asserted that the Nisga'a Lisims Government's power to limit political rights to non-Nisga'a was also unconstitutional. While the challenge to the treaty was similar to the *Campbell* case, the *Chief Mountain* case was construed more broadly. The *Chief Mountain* case challenged the treaty on the grounds that it violated fundamental rights enshrined in the Charter:

> The Agreement violates the Plaintiffs' right to Security of the Person pursuant to section 7 of the Charter by conferring on the Nisga'a Lisims Government the power to deny the right to vote and hold office in Nisga'a government.

> The Agreement violates the section 15 Charter right to be equal under the law in that part of Canada placed under the control of the Nisga'a Lisims Government by reason of the fact that essential rights exercisable therein by the Plaintiffs as Canadian citizens, such as citizenship, voting, job opportunities, taxation, and benefits, would be determined on the basis of laws based on race or ethnicity passed by a government whose constitution is based on race or ethnicity.[45]

This challenge, in contrast with the *Campbell* case, did not simply question the procedural propriety of the Nisga'a treaty under the Canadian Constitution, but challenged the fluid characterization of the Canadian Constitution that allowed the NFA to exist.

Launched in 2000, the *Chief Mountain* case initially made little progress. It was dismissed by the British Columbia Supreme Court for the failure of the plaintiffs to provide particulars as to the class of individuals whom it was being alleged were having their Charter rights violated, as Justice Cullen explained in the hearing where the respondents (the Nisga'a Nation et al.) requested the particulars of the claim.[46] The claim was dismissed on October 31, 2005, when these particulars were not provided. On appeal, Justice Saunders of the Court of Appeal revived the claim on October 9, 2007. The Supreme Court of British Columbia heard the case in October 2010 and concluded in early 2011.

The decision, released in October 2011, was rather anticlimactic. Justice Smith followed Justice Williamson's decision in the *Campbell* case on all issues raised in that previous matter. This judgement again confirms the interpretation of section 91 and 92 as non-exhaustive. In the alternative, Justice Smith found that the delegation of power to the Nisga'a Nation in the treaty was valid. She also affirms that section 35 indeed protects First Nation self-government, within limits:

> Following *Campbell*, I accept that the self-government powers in the NFA are protected by s. 35 of the *Constitution Act, 1982*. They are protected by s. 35 as treaty rights whether their source was delegation or an inherent Aboriginal right to self-government. As with other Aboriginal and treaty rights, they are not absolute; the federal and British Columbia governments would be able, in some circumstances, to infringe them. While it is unnecessary to define those circumstances in this case, it is possible that the Sparrow standard would be applied, permitting infringement where it is justified and consistent with the honour of the Crown.[47]

Indeed, the balance of the judgement was concerned with procedural issues and side-issues such as comity, collateral attack, justiciability, and standing.

There were two issues that were not previously decided in the *Campbell* case. This is the issue of the constitutionality of the taxation provisions in the treaty, and whether the administration of justice provisions violated section

96 of the *Constitution Act, 1867*. On the issue of taxes, Justice Smith held that Nisga'a taxation powers were valid as they were "expressly and unambiguously delegated to the Nisga'a Lisims Government . . . in order to raise revenue for Nisga'a Nation or Nisga'a Village purposes."[48] Though she also remarked that specific taxation legislation could potentially fall afoul of the Constitution, the specific law did not "fall within the scope of the delegated authority."[49] The provisions recognizing Nisga'a powers in relation to administration of justice were found not to violate section 96 of the Constitution on the grounds that the argument is still entirely speculative, as there are not currently any Nisga'a courts. The Nisga'a Lisims Government has not yet exercised its jurisdiction in relation to the administration of justice that could violate section 96. When the Nisga'a do invoke these provisions, they will be open to challenge.

The *Chief Mountain* case represented a profound legal challenge not only to the NFA, but to all the current and future comprehensive land claim treaties in Canada. It is too early to know if this decision will be appealed, but if it is and the Supreme Court takes a narrow interpretation of the Constitution, it is possible that all the legal groundwork underlying Aboriginal claims for self-government could be threatened. If the powers enumerated within section 91 and 92 are interpreted as the exhaustive and exclusive domain of the federal and provincial governments, much of the flawed, but fundamental gains for Aboriginal rights in Canada may be lost. If the Canadian Constitution is recognized to operate to extinguish independent Aboriginal claims for legitimacy, a liberal and limited interpretation of Aboriginal rights will prevail.

In my view, we have gone too far down the road of comprehensive land claims for the courts to intervene and undermine the entire basis for treaty making. In *Chief Mountain,* Justice Smith cites Justice Binnie in *Beckman* v. *Little Salmon/Carmacks First Nation,*[50] where he explains that modern comprehensive treaties must be treated with deference:

> Where adequately resourced and professionally represented parties have sought to order their own affairs, and have given shape to the duty to consult by incorporating consultation procedures into a treaty, their efforts should be encouraged and, subject to such constitutional limitations as the honour of the Crown, the Court should strive to respect their handiwork: Quebec (Attorney General) v. Moses, 2010 SCC 17, [2010] 1 S.C.R. 557.[51]

Rather than relying on contorted liberalism to understand the spectre of modern comprehensive land claims, it is my view that postcolonial theory can allow us to accept that Aboriginal self-determination is not just a step toward a positive future, but a necessary one. This sentiment is not entirely novel. Duncan Ivison argues for a model of constitutional postcolonialism that allows for the potential for recognition of Aboriginal sovereignty within more flexible interpretive regimes:

> What would a truly postcolonial interpretive regime look like, given the political and legal materials at hand? Legal and political regimes take Aboriginal claims seriously, I want to argue, in so far as they give the greatest amount of space possible for Aboriginal communities to negotiate their protection from, and engagement with, the wider political community. The question then is not the degree to which Aboriginal sovereignty can mimic the national sovereignty (once) exercised by nation-states. Their sovereignty, existing prior to and independent of European forms, is not reducible to those categories (nor explainable by them), though it is coordinate with them. . . .
>
> The legislative competence and supremacy of Parliament is, of course, already subject to various limitations in Australia given the federal structure. In so far as federalism is a "regime of multiple loyalties," the challenge is to adapt and accommodate this "legislative (omni) competence" to Aboriginal aspirations, and the recognition of a more diverse body of law.[52]

Ivison, therefore, imagines a constitutionalism that can include independent Aboriginal legal legitimacy within the existing structure. The *Campbell* case represents this type of postcolonial vision of open-textured constitutionalism, where Aboriginal sovereignty can be a component part. If this interpretation is adopted, the NFA and all other treaties in Canada are safe from being declared illegitimate.

Other commentators, however, have proposed a more pessimistic interpretation of the legal determination of Aboriginal rights and its potential for instantiating Aboriginal justice that maintains its oppressive colonial connotations. Stuart Motha, is of the view that the law has "difficulty . . . freeing itself of the violence of origin." He explains, in relation to the *Mabo* case, that within the existing colonial legal structures Aboriginal difference can never be recognized. While he ultimately advocates that "[b]oth Aboriginal and non-aboriginal people need to explore much more flexible and temporary categories and concepts for resolving the conundrum of recognizing difference,"[53] existing law is limited by its inherent inability to recognize difference:

> Recognizing that knowledge is relative to the standpoint of the knower is not the end of the matter. The limits of knowledge can be supplemented by dialogue. Non-Aboriginal people can, to a limited extent, know what lies beyond their knowledge by listening to what Aboriginal people have to say. What is understood through dialogue may never amount to actual understanding. However, it may enable non-Aboriginal people to cease the practices that do actual harm to Aboriginal people and facilitate the emergence of a relationship that allows Aboriginal people to realize their self-determined aspirations. The possibility of this closed off when concepts like "native title" or a property right are introduced as the mediating device for the relationship between the two groups. The possibilities then become finite and the dialogue becomes deadlocked. This is evident in the current climate where the debate is dominated by the conditions of extinguishment of "native title."[54]

These observations echo the criticisms of the NFA provided by Canadian academics such as Paul Rynard.[55] Once the Nisga'a formalized their rights and power into a treaty, according to this account, they become mere shadows of Aboriginal "otherness" that will ultimately fail to live up to the project of decolonization. The treaty becomes another clever colonial tactic for assimilation. There therefore, in a broad characterization, seem to be two different theoretical perspectives on the treaty. The first recognizes it as a development toward a postcolonial constitutionalism, which has the potential to express First Nations' aspirations. The second discounts such efforts as another failure to adequately recognize the extent of Aboriginal difference within an unchallengeable sovereignty.

Through examining the dynamics of the *Chief Mountain* challenge, I would argue that we can see that potentially damaging effect of the latter theoretical perspective. While there may be little progress in the legal system, Chief Mountain's counsel are actively lobbying for support (mainly financial) in the political arena. In the 28 November 2008 edition of the *Canadian Journal of Ideas* (C2C), John Carpay has published an article attacking the treaty on several grounds. These grounds include the constitutional issues alleged in both the *Campbell* and the *Chief Mountain* challenges discussed above. The allegation most relevant to this exploration, however, is the assertion that the NFA creates an "illiberal Constitution." Ultimately, this is a challenge to a treaty that makes "some Canadians have different rights and different legal status based on ancestry, descent or ethnicity."[56] This may indeed be an illiberal notion; however, as I have argued, liberalism should not be viewed as an unchangeable set of normative truths to be universally applied in all contexts. Indeed, this is the most insidious inheritance of colonialism. John D. Weston, in furtherance to the same cause, has argued:

> Community ownership of most property is inferior to private ownership, Mr. Gibson argued, echoing Hernando DeSoto. Mr. Gibson conceded that the choice of collective ownership ought to be there for Indians who want it, but merely proposed that the model not be assumed as exclusive. Chief Gosnell's vision is squarely at odds with that of Mr. Gibson on this matter. Under the Nisga'a Treaty, certain core lands, like traditional reserve lands, are Nisga'a Territory, and cannot be alienated. [57]

This argument clearly aligns the challenge to the treaty with the dominant liberal values of Canadian society. It is difficult to see how, considering the liberal opposition to the treaty, if Chief Mountain wins his claim any First Nation would be able to assert the right to self-determination.

The critiques emanating from critical theory ultimately confirm the dominance of the existing system, and reinforce a political and constitutional interpretation that excludes the possibility of First Nations negotiating material rights within it. If indeed, no constellation of hybrid property right is sufficient to instantiate Aboriginal difference, we are left with the stark polarities of the liberal annihilation of negotiated treaties, or a reaching to understand difference that is "beyond [and] may never be reached."[58] While arguments such as Motha's are useful to remind us that we must always strive to keep expanding our limited European assumptions in the face of Aboriginal difference, this discourse may threaten the expansion of notions of sovereignty and constitutionalism that we have witnessed in the *Campbell* case.

If one looks beyond the liberal arguments that are being advanced by counsel in the *Chief Mountain* matter, however, there is a more meaningful interpretation of the challenge. In the interviews I conducted in the Nass Valley, there were members of the Nation that expressed discontent with the situation that emerged from the Nisga'a Final Agreement. As one member of the Nisga'a Nation expressed it, traditional Nisga'a society had been irrevocably changed by the treaty. In this member's view, the treaty has exacerbated the gap between the rich and the poor. The centralizing of power in a government in Gitlaxt'aamiks (New Aiyansh), according to this member, has resulted in a different order of government with Nisga'a who had "gone out to get an education coming back to be big shots, who don't get out on the land." This member thought that the current leadership was "changing the culture to suit their needs." What these discussions seemed to suggest, in the limited perception of an outside observer, is that while the NFA can be seen as a significant milestone in the recognition of First Nations, it also presents an extraordinary challenge for the Nisga'a people. To return to Chief Mountain, he has been reported as saying,

> The Chief Mountain of centuries past would have fought to the death to preserve his ancestral lands and his people's rights. I inherited a heavy responsibility. I have no choice but to fight in the courtrooms to preserve my culture, as the Nisga'a Government is a dictatorial form of government. There is no opposition party. If anyone speaks against their actions, the speakers are ostracized. I am prepared to stake all that I have on this because it will erode my culture, my traditions, our way of life, and the future of our children yet unborn. The courts are supposed to channel these disputes away from physical violence and yet I'm being prevented even from getting to trial.[59]

At the heart of this challenge seems to be an expression that the changes invoked by the NFA are inconsistent with the cultural values Chief Mountain wants to protect.

This challenge also has to do with land. One article stated,

> If he succeeds, any actions based on the Treaty would also be invalid, and must be reversed. Chief Mountain says his ancestral lands and many other Nisga'a lands were surrendered by the Nisga'a negotiators in exchange for unconstitutional authority that gave them great power — but power they were never eligible to have. He wants his lands back, and he does not want to be subject to an aboriginal government with powers that cut him off from the benefits of Canadian Citizenship. As he says in an affidavit: "I am Canadian."[60]

Where it becomes difficult to disentangle Chief Mountain's claim is when counsel involved argue against concepts such as communal ownership. As Weston has written, "community ownership of most property is inferior to private ownership. . . . the choice of collective ownership ought to be there for Indians who want it, but merely proposed that the model not be assumed as exclusive."[61] While it does seem clear that Chief Mountain is not happy with the political order the NFA has instituted, it is a matter of speculation whether the political order he desires is possible with the arguments being made by his liberal allies in his legal claim.

Conclusion

The *Campbell* decision represents a remarkable evolution of Canadian sovereignty. This is a sovereignty that is limited by its own Constitution, not empowered by it. First Nations are recognized in terms that would be unthinkable in earlier jurisprudence, and accepted as legitimate governing authorities within the Canadian state. Indeed, in the *Campbell* case, sovereignty is not the authority that validates power; rather, it is the exercise of power that instantiates sovereignty. This case rewrites that narrative of sovereignty in Canada. While previously, a European power planting a flag, either literally or figuratively, constituted the unilateral assertion of a sovereignty of administrative, political, and social dominance, Canadian sovereignty is now one that recognizes the continuing right to self-determination within an evolving state.

This is not where the story ends, however. It continues as First Nations, deprived of political rights in Canada until 1960, are recognized as semi-sovereign "third-order" governments within Canada. The debate now is whether the means by which the Nisga'a Nation has been recognized truly reflects Nisga'a culture. While this debate within Nisga'a society could be interpreted as a reflection that the Nisga'a Final Agreement is simply another colonial strategy to incorporate Aboriginal peoples into mainstream colonial culture, the discursive strategies being used to challenge the treaty suggest that the treaty actually is a threat to dominant liberal Canadian values. A postcolonial view would instead see the debate as the continuing process of postcolonial production. It is easy to interpret postcolonial theory as only the experience of the colonizer. If, however, we perceive postcolonialism as a process of cultural engagement not limited to a colonial dialectic, a different analysis emerges. Homi Bhabha writes,

Terms of cultural engagement, whether antagonistic or affiliate, are produced performatively. The representation of difference must not be hastily read as the reflection of pre-given ethnic or cultural traits set in a fixed tablet of tradition. The social articulation of difference, from the minority perspective, is a complex on-going negotiation that seeks to authorize cultural hybridities that emerge in moments of historical transformation. The "right" to signify from the periphery of authorized power and privilege does not depend on the persistence of tradition; it is resourced by the power of tradition to be reinscribed through the conditions of contingency and contradictoriness that attend upon the lives of those who are "in the minority." The recognition that tradition bestows a partial form of identification. In restaging the past it introduces other, incommensurable cultural temporalities into the invention of tradition. This process estranges any immediate access to an originary identity or "received" tradition. The borderline engagements of cultural difference may as often be consensual as conflictual; they may confound our definitions of traditional and modernity; realign the customary boundaries between the private and the public, high and low; and challenge normative expectations of development and progress.[62]

Whilst this passage can be read as the process that the "colonizer" is faced with which destabilizes their understandings of progress, modernity, and identity, Chief Mountain's challenge suggests that we should interpret this passage as the process that colonized people also experience in the postcolonial world. A postcolonial perspective will never provide the answer to cultural engagements either between or within, but possibly it can inform how both the colonizer and the colonized can understand the experience of "how, in motion, in transition, in movement, you must continually build a habitation for your ideas, your thoughts, and yourself."[63]

If current theoretical articles on the postcolonial suggest anything, it is that postcolonial does not signal, in the end, a theoretical, or indeed the practical, endeavour. It instead seems simply to signal a different and more complex starting point. This chapter demonstrates that this is the reality, politically as well as theoretically. While Canadian constitutionalism has undergone a remarkable revision, Chief Mountain's challenge to the treaty suggests that it is not only the Canadian political and legal community that are experiencing anxiety about the postcolonial present. The Nisga'a are also struggling to accommodate the negotiated resolution in the NFA.

◯

CHAPTER SIX

Conclusion: Postcolonial Sovereignty?

Now this is not the end. It is not even the beginning of the end. But it is, perhaps, the end of the beginning.

Sir Winston Churchill (November 10, 1942)

Introduction

Canada is not the only country in the world struggling to reconcile national minority claims for land and sovereignty with a notion of sovereignty built on the foundations of a colonial and imperial past. In all populated continents, governments are left struggling with the legacy of a world order founded upon the belief that certain cultural groups had the inherent right to rule (and exploit) all others. The question of how we are to move out from under the shadow of a believed european superiority[1] into a more inclusive global society is the most important challenge we face in the twenty-first century.

At present, it is my fear that this challenge is being approached in an unnecessarily simplistic manner. It seems that there is a view that reconciliation of these deep tensions must result in complete abdication of power or absolute independence. One is radically alterior or assimilated; subjugated or conqueror; slave or master. It has been my aim in this book to suggest that the polarized discourse of sovereignty does not adequately account for the actual productive life of culture, law, and governance. As Henderson has said, "theory and reasoning are supposed to help us understand the diversity of the world, not be a substitute for it."[2] Perhaps a more nuanced theory is necessary.

The Limits of Liberalism?

Liberalism, and particularly liberal equality, has emerged as a central mantra of Western european political theory. In chapter one, I suggested that there is an intense discomfort where self-government agreements challenge this central tenet of Canadian political life. Certainly, the Charter[3] has brought in an era of substantive rather than formal equality; it has not, however, resulted in the endorsement of independent, ethnically based national minorities within the Canadian state. Comprehensive land claims and self-government agreements go beyond what Charter rights can recognize. Comprehensive claims and self-government agreements politically recognize that the First Nations of Canada deserve recognition politically, culturally, socially, and economically.

In chapter one, I argued that, with the Nisga'a Final Agreement, we have reached the limits of liberal accommodation, and that a different analysis is now necessary. I argued that a postcolonial framework provides some insights into how we can understand First Nation governance in contemporary Canada — through understanding culture, history, and power differently. Putting liberalism aside for the moment, let us just think about the narrative of Western settlement of North America. The story, very simplistically, is that europeans showed up and imposed order on a vast blank green canvas while Indigenous peoples struggled to adapt to the new world order. The ending of this story was always that Indigenous people adapt to the new world order and — eureka! — we have the future. This is an admittedly oversimplified but not so inaccurate story of the founding of Canada.

This narrative is fiction, at best. Western "civilized" culture has been treating Aboriginals as children in need of education and protection for over a century. It has been under the auspices of this narrative that a program of assimilation was maintained for over two hundred years. In a discussion with one member of the Nisga'a Nation, she commented that maybe it is Western civilization that has been the children. She said that "we have always been here, maybe now [Canadian society] has grown up enough to be able to listen to us." Possibly it is our time to listen, and revise the myth of our origins.

This story of North American settlement, and its continued acceptance, is predicated on the belief that european understandings of the world are 1) inherently correct, and 2) unassailable. I would like to think that, at least in the academic and political sphere, we have accepted that european superiority is an absurd fiction that has masqueraded as the justification for the exploitation of peoples around the world. Possibly this is naïve, but such is the nature of my optimism. The underlying belief I have tried to address in this book is that european cultural, political, and social norms are unassailable. In very basic terms, there is the belief that Canadian law and society either cannot change to incorporate First Nations, or that even if they can we are not really sure we want them to. What this book has been arguing is that, whether we like it or not, we are changing as the result of the participation of First Nations. The thirty years of political negotiation for First Nation self-government has changed Canadian society. The constitutional conferences on Aboriginal self-government modified Canadian political values. Oka, Nunavut, the Royal Commission on Aboriginal Peoples, the British Columbia Treaty Commission,[4] and all the modern comprehensive land claims have all been slowly changing Canadian law and society. We are, not as Saul suggested, already a Métis nation[5]; we are in the process of becoming a Métis nation.

This is the relevance of postcolonial theory. It allows us to view the world as it is becoming, not simply as what it once was. It is easy to buy into the myth of european superiority if all we do is look at relationships and power through the lens of the master/slave narrative.[6] If, however, we perceive the world through the complex and competing networks of power that are constantly influencing the direction of our future, it is not so easy. On these terms, postcolonial theory can provide us with a "middle way." This middle way does not provide the answers to the daily social, legal, and political challenges that colonialism has created, but rather provides us with a mode of analysis that may allow us to avoid the prison of an unyielding Western theory. Indeed, postcolonial theory may provide us with the key to open the cell doors and emerge from the fetters of outdated european epistemologies. As John Bird writes about Aboriginal sovereignty and the future of Canada, "[n]othing is as it was before. That can be threatening. But it is also what we find exciting and hopeful about this period of history."[7] Postcolonial theory may "bring back to light the midwife of history,"[8] to use Sartre's description of Fanon's engagement with colonialism. History is constantly being made in the constant and inevitable production of the future. Discourse is language that makes this history. One only has to look at the effect that Martin Luther King, Nelson Mandela, and Harold Cardinal have had to recognize that fact.

While the effect of these leaders is a very obvious manifestation of discourse making history, the effect of the Nisga'a Nation through the NFA is no less significant. Its operation is more nuanced, however. This treaty has affirmed Nisga'a sovereignty within the Canadian constitutional framework. It has created an elaborate power-sharing arrangement that can further facilitate the meaningful participation of the Nisga'a Nation within Canada and the world. It has validated the Nisga'a right to self-determination within Canadian law and politics. This may create more questions than answers, such as how effectively the Nisga'a can exercise this sovereignty within the existing bureaucracy. This will be discussed at more length later in this chapter.

In chapter two, I argued that the land provisions in the NFA create a hybrid version of landholding that is neither traditionally Aboriginal nor Western. This model of landholding uses legal concepts familiar to the Canadian landholding system, yet implements characteristics of Aboriginal landholding fundamental to the ongoing survival of the Nisga'a Nation. Critics would contest this statement, arguing that the ability of the Nisga'a to sell Nisga'a land to non-Nisga'a is a threat to the Nisga'a Nation.

This concern has been heightened by the passing of the *Nisga'a Landholding Transition Act* in 2009.[9] This Act allows for Nisga'a citizens to acquire land in fee simple. This has sparked concern about the erosion of the Nisga'a land base. Nelson Leeson, then President of the NLG, described the move rather differently. He stated that "[t]his is a significant step towards true self government. It is a process for increasing economic prosperity for our people. It is important for us to be able to find ways of building capacity for our people so that they can stand on their own."[10] He is referring here to the ability of the Nisga'a to use their land as collateral for loans to generate capital. It should be remembered, however, that whoever owns the land, it remains subject to Nisga'a laws, including zoning and building regulations.

Ultimately, it must be remembered that the right to self-determination entails more than simply the right to have access to resources constrained by the modern idea of traditional pre-contact practices; it means that the Nisga'a Nation can choose how to use their territory to support modern Nisga'a culture. If this includes the ability for Nisga'a lands to become security for modern economic activities, then so be it. Ultimately, the NFA should not be dismissed as the extension of colonial power over the Nisga'a or seen as a unilateral victory. Instead, the treaty should be seen as a milestone in the inevitable evolution of both Canadian and Nisga'a cultures produced through engagement.

In chapter three, I argued that the NFA provisions relating to resources has implemented a model that cannot be described as merely an accommodation within a liberal model through examining other Aboriginal "rights" in the NFA. Nisga'a "rights" under the NFA far exceed the model of historical rights proposed in *Van der Peet*[11] or *Pamajewon*.[12] The NFA not only recognizes historical Nisga'a rights; it recognizes Nisga'a power. If we think back to Kymlicka's rationalization of national minority accommodation, this type of power cannot be justified through appeals to equality. Indeed, the NFA explicitly recognizes that the Nisga'a deserve not only a share of valuable resources; they also deserve power to decide how these resources are used (or not).

The NFA also recognizes powers far beyond an understanding of Nisga'a culture as a fixed list of historical ceremonies and food harvesting methods. The NFA recognizes that the Nisga'a are a modern, living culture. When asked how the NFA has affected Nisga'a culture, the typical response was that "the culture is what it is." The Nisga'a aren't so much interested in preserving their culture (definition: protecting it from anything that would cause its current quality or condition to change), as they are interested in providing opportunities for it to evolve and flourish. A postcolonial understanding of culture would suggest that we should look at all cultures this way, rather than believing there is some "authentic" Indian, or Ukrainian, or Englishman. Postcolonial theory urges us to understand these discordances as products of the sometimes affiliative and sometimes agonistic engagements between cultures, which produces something that may be "new" but are still "resourced by the power of tradition."[13]

A closer analysis of the resource provisions also demonstrates that, while it might be correct to characterize Nisga'a claims as a claim for power, it would be more appropriate to characterize their claims as a claim for responsibility over the resources that are so fundamental to their survival, both economically and culturally. In the struggle for national self-determination there often seems to be little thought of the responsibilities that correspond with this independence. However, as the political situation in Somalia demonstrates as drought ravages the Horn of Africa, it is the responsibilities of governance that need to be more seriously considered. As this human tragedy unfolds, it is becoming clearer that no national government — even the most powerful — can stand entirely on its own, and refrain from being, in some way, dependent upon others. The ongoing global recessions that have been plaguing even the largest global economic players from the near economic collapse of Greece, Ireland, and Portugal illustrate how interconnected every nation is. This dependence cannot be subjection, however; it has to be co-operation. As the results of the uprisings in Egypt, Tunisia, and Libya — the "Arab spring" — unfold, it is my fervent hope that the creation of a new sense of nationhood will take into its genesis the lessons of the new global postcolonial world. It is entirely possible that nationhood is always a negotiation between independence and compromise. If it is possible for us to exorcise the colonial superiority that has characterized the past several centuries, and instead understand tolerance as not just accepting what we can understand, but most importantly, accepting what we do not, then it may be possible to build a better human community sourced from the strength of our differences. The lesson we learn from the Nisga'a is that power means responsibility, and this responsibility should be taken very seriously.

In chapter four, I examined the nuts and bolts of self-determination in the treaty. The NFA is not as simple a document as the American *Declaration of Independence*. It is not simply statements of autonomy.[14] The NFA is a nuanced, detailed, and complicated delineation of authority over a detailed list of resources and responsibilities. It is a statement of Nisga'a autonomy combined with the type of provisions found in complex international treaties. It is somewhat reminiscent of the detailed treaties that have allowed the creation of the European Union as a political and economic unit.[15] An absolute notion of "sovereignty," therefore, is not relevant to the NFA. We need instead to look at the complex arena of international relations to find its parallels.

In chapter five, I examined the judicial reception of the NFA. In the *Campbell* and *Chief Mountain* cases, the courts have affirmed that the NFA has become clothed with the same protection as the Canadian government and its sovereignty. Sovereignty is sometime characterized as unchallengeable, its source unquestionable. The *Campbell* case demonstrates that the NFA is now protected by the same inviolability as Canadian sovereignty. The NFA, and the powers of the Nisga'a government within this interpretation, rather than being excluded by it, have been afforded the protection of Canadian sovereignty. As a basic illustration, prior to the treaty, the Nisga'a Nation and the federal or provincial government were sitting at opposing tables. Nisga'a legal counsel now sit at the same table as the federal and provincial governments. This is a remarkable reversal.

Postcolonial Sovereignty?

The question at the heart of this book is whether a postcolonial sovereignty is possible, and whether the NFA indeed represents such a development. The preceding analysis of the treaty at least crystallizes what the real questions are that are necessary to begin answering this question. First, can a national sovereignty (in this case, Canada) embrace self-determining First Nations within its political and constitutional framework? Second, can this self-determination be effectively and meaningfully exercised within it? Tacitly, the answer to both questions is yes. Unfortunately, the answers to such questions are never that simple.

Before I can begin to discuss these questions, as with any discussion relating to contested political and theoretical concepts, it is incumbent upon me to try to explain what I mean by a postcolonial sovereignty. A postcolonial sovereignty would be an idea of nationhood that is not organized on the logic of colonial oppression. What this means is that the nation cannot operate upon principles of european cultural (legal, linguistic, social) superiority. A description that I find most illustrative is Tuitt's discussion in *Race, Law and Resistance*.[16] Her description of the postcolonial project suggests that the "founding myths" of the nation have to be revised, rewritten, and re-inscribed in the legal and institutional culture. John Ralston Saul's book, *A Fair Country*,[17] is an example of such a revision, where he argues that the founding myths of Canada have omitted the influence of Aboriginal peoples in the development of Canada as a nation. This requires the revision of everything from the *Constitution*[18] (which has been achieved to some degree) to the modification of institutional bureaucracy to effectively include First Nations. This brings us back to the question of whether Canada can embrace self-determining First Nations, and how this self-determination can be exercised within the complex political arrangements in Canada.

The first burning question is whether Canada can accept self-determining First Nations within its political and constitutional framework. The short answer is yes. Our Constitution enshrines and protects Aboriginal and treaty rights in section 35. When this provision was included in the Constitution, self-government was considered to fall somehow within these rights. The issue was how to implement self-government. While these particular discussions may have been omitted from Canadian collective memory, this provision was brought in with the express contemplation of some form of First Nation self-government in mind.

The reason why the answer to this question is not so simple lies in our deep allegiance to liberal principles that abhor any principle that could compromise the perception of equality. My first observation is that liberal sovereignty openly accepts inequality. Simply ask a new immigrant to this country if Canadian citizenship is so egalitarian. Sovereign nations always maintain the right to exclude people from the protection and benefits of society. Simply because First Nations have been living within the borders that we have called Canada does not mean that they should not also maintain that right. It may be that we haven't yet found the appropriate relationship to welcome First Nations into the Canadian confederation as equal and participating members.

Another concern, as expressed by Kymlicka, is that by having self-governing ethnic minorities within a liberal state we somehow will lose our notion of a Canadian identity. If Canadian history teaches us anything, this concern is not well founded. As John Ibbitson has observed, Canada is a successful state because we are a failed nation. Canada has never coalesced as a unified nation. As Ibbitson has argued, Canada's multiculturalism policies have created a truly post-national state. In his opinion, Canada "owe[s] our success as a country to our failure as a nation. To repeat: Canada never really had a chance to gel as a nation-state because the French and English divide was too pronounced."[19] As a result, he says,

> Our lack of national homogeneity, which has reduced Canada to a lowest common denominator of statehood, inculcated in the country an acceptance of diversity and a respect for minority sensibilities unmatched by any other place on the planet. Immigrants integrated more easily into the fabric of the society because the design of the garment was a mosaic, a patchwork quilt that welcomed and was enriched by new patches. And the absence of a dominant national culture made it easier to assimilate immigrants, since there was nothing all that intimidating for them to assimilate into.[20]

Surely, if we apply this logic to First Nations, the meaningful inclusion of First Nations in Canadian political and legal life is long overdue. Principles are ultimately good. Liberalism does provide us with some reasonable principles upon which we can organize our collective lives. This does not mean that these principles should never be re-evaluated or attenuated.

The next question is whether this self-determination can be effectively and meaningfully exercised within Canada. One might expect the answer to be yes. There are multiple provisions in the NFA that require co-management of resources. One might think that this would be easy. The experience of the Nisga'a Nation has not been such. It was explained to me that while treaty negotiations were ongoing, the Nisga'a Nation had an open line to the provincial and federal governments. Once the treaty was signed, however, communication was limited to lower-level bureaucrats in the Department of Indian Affairs and Northern Development (DIAND). The same bureaucracy that manages Indians under the *Indian Act*[21] has been given the task of intergovernmental relations. The result of this delegation is that the same bureaucracy that has been administering Indians under the existing paternalistic system is now in charge of participating in a nation-to-nation relationship. This arrangement does not honour the spirit of the agreement.

The need to change the structure of the federal bureaucracy in relation to Aboriginal peoples in Canada should come as no surprise. This was one of the many recommendations in the Royal Commission on Aboriginal Peoples. RCAP recommended that DIAND be abolished and replaced by a Department of Aboriginal Affairs and a Department of Indian and Inuit Services.[22] Alongside the creation of new departments, RCAP recommended that

the prime minister appoint in a new senior cabinet position a minister of Aboriginal relations, to be responsible for
- guiding all federal actions associated with fully developing and implementing the new federal/Aboriginal relationship, which forms the core of this Commission's recommendations;
- allocating funds from the federal government's total Aboriginal expenditures across the government; and
- the activity of the chief Crown negotiator responsible for the negotiation of treaties, claims and self-government accords.[23]

Further, they recommended the creation of a new Aboriginal Affairs Cabinet Committee.[24] It was suggested that these reforms be implemented within a year of the report being published.[25] Over ten years and numerous comprehensive land claims and self-government treaties later, these recommendations have not yet been implemented.[26] If "[c]omplying with this deadline" was supposed to "send a clear signal that the government of Canada not only intends to reform its fundamental relationship with Aboriginal peoples but is taking the first practical steps to do so,"[27] the signs are not good. Possibly it is politics. Possibly it is simply the inertia of institutionalized bureaucracy. Regardless, in order for First Nations to exercise self-government effectively, the federal and provincial governments are going to have to ensure that there are effective political mechanisms to engage in a nation-to-nation relationship. Imagine if the prime minister of the U.K. had to leave messages on the voicemail of a mid-level policy official in order to discuss the implementation of international economic treaties. First Nations who have equivalent international agreements should not be treated this way.

Conclusion

The NFA does indeed represent a movement toward a "postcolonial sovereignty." Postcolonialism is always a process spurred on by the uncomfortable and irreconcilable cultural tensions inherent in a complex and diverse world. Through developing the idea of a postcolonial sovereignty, however, I do not want to detract from the real initiatives and transformations that are occurring across Canada. As James Youngblood Henderson writes,

> Those who hold power have categorized our efforts to transform their texts into documents of inclusion and empowerment for Indigenous peoples as "postcolonial legal thought." I enjoy the inspirational idea of "postcolonial," but achieving this state is still problematic. The legal and academic positivists insist on forging a definition of the concept of postcolonialism to place in their word dictionary and debate its meanings. Indigenous lawyers and scholars, however, conceptualize the idea as discursive remedies to our suffering, rather than quibbling word games and conceptual riddles as in Eurocentrism. The remedies in are in our vision, consciousness, and feelings. They remain in the places and ceremonies that our Creator placed them; it is for us to continually rediscover and renew those teachings.[28]

It is truly the efforts for cultural and economic renewal in First Nations communities across Canada that are responsible for the transformation of Canadian law and governance. In the introduction to a new edition of Sartre's *Colonialism and Neocolonialism,* Robert Young writes that Fanon's work, *Black Skin, White Masks,* is a liberatory text because "the colonial subject constantly oscillates between the two states, internalizing the colonial ideology of inferiority and being less than fully human — until he, or she, assumes responsibility and chooses authenticity and freedom."[29] This is a good description of the process Aboriginal people have been undergoing. They are assuming responsibility for their communities, and choosing authenticity and freedom. It is my view that Canadians should embrace this new relationship, and not allow philosophical shackles to frustrate First Nation self-determination. In the Red Paper, Harold Cardinal wrote:

> What the Indian wants is really quite simple. He wants the chance to develop the resources available to him on his own homeland, the re-

serve. What he needs to make this possible includes financial assistance, enough money to do the job properly so that he does not fail for lack of adequate financing; training in the precise skills he will need to develop the resources, training so practical and appropriate to the task that he will not fail because he does not have the know-how to do the job and, finally, access to expert advice and counsel throughout the stages of development so that he will not fail because he was given the wrong advice or no advice at all. With the money, the know-how and expert guidance, then if the Indian fails, at least it will not be because he didn't try to succeed and at least it will not be because he was not allowed to try.

One key factor remains, Indian involvement. Our people want the right to set their own goals, determine their own priorities, create and stimulate their own opportunities and development. The government knows this. This is part of what we have whispered, talked and screamed about. But the government mind, once on a path, seems difficult to divert. Once a government bureaucrat makes up his mind, there is no point trying to change it with logic and facts. And the government long ago decided it knew what was best for its Indian charges.[30]

The NFA gives the Nisga'a the power to set their own goals, make their own priorities, and develop the opportunities they decide upon. It is not certain where this treaty, and others of its kind will lead us in the future. It is fair to say, however, that the signing of the NFA is not where the story ends, but where the story of the possibility of a more fair, just, and inclusive Canada begins.

Notes

Notes to Introduction

1   *Delgamuukw* v. *British Columbia*, [1997] 3 S.C.R. 1010 at para 81.

2   See P. Fitzpatrick, "'We Know What It Is When You Do Not Ask Us': The Un-challengable Nation" (2004). *Finnish Yearbook of International Law* XV: 144.

3   See J. Weston, "National Implications of Chief Mountain's Challenge to the Third Order of Government and the Nisga'a Treaty"; www.reformbc.net/news2003/Feb19_03.pdf. See also T. Flanagan, *First Nations? Second Thoughts* (Montreal: McGill-Queens University Press, 2000).

4   C. Denis, "Indigenous Citizenship and History in Canada: Between Denial and Imposition," in R. Adamoski, D. Chunn, and R. Menzies (Eds.), *Contesting Canadian Citizenship: Historical Readings* (Peterborough: Broadview Press, 2002) at 13.

5   H. Cardinal, *The Unjust Society* (Edmonton: M. G. Hurtig Ltd, 1969).

6   *Ibid.* at 17.

7   *Calder* v. *British Columbia*, (1973), 34 D.L.R. (3d) 145.

8   *Delgamuukw* v. *British Columbia* (1997) 3 S.C.R. 1010 (S.C.C.).

9   DIAND, "Statement Made by the Honourable Jean Chrétien Minister of Indian Affairs and Northern Development on Claims of Indian and Inuit People: *Communique*, 8 Aug. 1973.

10 Aboriginal Affairs and Northern Development Canada, "General Briefing Note on Canada's Self–Government and Land Claims Policies and the Status of Negotiations January 2011"; www.ainc-inac.gc.ca/al/ldc/ccl/pubs/gbn/gbn-eng.asp#section1.

11 House of Commons, *Special Committee on Indian Self-Government in Canada: Report of the Special Committee* ("Penner Report," 1983).

12 E. R. Atleo, *Tsawalk: A Nuu-chah-nulth Worldview* (Vancouver: UBC Press, 2004) at 67.

13 Canada, British Columbia & the Nisga'a Nation, *Nisga'a Final Agreement & Appendices*; www.gov.bc.ca/arr/firstnation/nisgaa/default.html#.

14 The Nisga'a Lisims Government (NLG) is the name for the central authority in the Nisga'a Nation government. "Lisims" in the Nisga'a language is the name for the Nass River.

15 *Supra* note 5 at 64.

Notes to Chapter 1

1   G. Gaus and S. D. Courtland, "Liberalism," *The Stanford Encyclopedia of Philosophy* (Spring 2011 Edition), N. Z. Edward (Ed.); http://plato.stanford.edu/archives/spr2011/entries/liberalism/.

2   See, e.g., C. Taylor, *Reconciling the Solitudes: Essays on Canadian Federalism and Nationalism* (Montreal: Queen's University Press, 1993); "The Politics of Recognition" in A. Gutmann (Ed.), *Multiculturalism* (Princeton: Princeton University Press, 1994); and J. Tully, *Strange multiplicity: Constitutionalism in an age of diversity* (Cambridge: Cambridge University Press, 1995).

3   W. Kymlicka, *Liberalism, Community and Culture* (Oxford: Clarendon Press, 1989).

4   W. Kymlicka, *Multicultural Citizenship: A Liberal Theory if Minority Rights* (Oxford: Clarendon Press, 1995).

5   J. Y. Henderson, "Postcolonial Indigenous Legal Consciousness" (2002), *Indigenous Law Journal*, Vol. 1, Spring 2002.

6   H. K. Bhabha, *The Location of Culture* (London: Routledge, 1994).

7   E. W. Said, *Orientalism: Western Representations of the Orient* (Harmondsworth: Penguin, 1978).

8   *Supra* note 3 at 13.

9   *Ibid.* at 1.

10   *Ibid.*

11   *Ibid.* at 13.

12   *Supra* note 4 at 255.

13   *Ibid.* at 11.

14   *Ibid.* at 30.

15   *Ibid.* at 31.

16   While historically there would not be full acceptance of this in some circles, it is now a fairly accepted political and legal fact in Canada that First Nations were sovereign peoples prior to European settlement.

17   *Supra* note 4 at 31.

18   *Ibid.*

19   *Ibid.* at 109–10.

20   *Ibid.*

21 *Ibid.*

22 *Ibid.* at 76.

23 *Ibid.* at 77.

24 *Ibid.* at 116–20.

25 *Ibid.* at 117

26 *Ibid.* at 118.

27 *St. Catherine's Milling and Lumber Co.* v. *R.* (1889) 2 C.N.L.C. 541 (J.C.P.C.).

28 *Ibid.* at 549.

29 *Canada Act, 1982* (U.K.) 1982, c. 11.

30 See, e.g., *Royal Proclamation*, 1763 (U.K.), 14 Geo. III, c. 83.

31 The balance of section 35(1) and (2) defines Aboriginal people and the rights that can be acquire by future treaties.

32 See P. Fitzpatrick, "'We Know What It Is When You Do Not Ask Us': The Unchallengable Nation" (2004) *Finnish Yearbook of International Law XV*, 129. In this article, Fitzpatrick uses the *Van der Peet* case as an example of how the unchallengable "instantiated sovereign seeks to encompass and embody right" (144) in his argument about the sacred instantiation of the determinate nation.

33 *Van der Peet* v. *R.* [1996] 2 S.C.R. 507 at para. 49.

34 *Ibid.* at para 50.

35 *Ibid.* at para 43.

36 *Ibid.*

37 *Ibid.* at para 91.

38 R. L. Barsh & J. Y. Henderson, "The Supreme Court's *Van der Peet* Trilogy: Naïve Imperialism and Ropes of Sand" (1997) 42 *McGill L.J.* 994 at 1002.

39 *Ibid.* at 1000.

40 *Ibid.* at 1001.

41 *Ibid.*

42 See B. W. Morse, "Permafrost Rights: Aboriginal Self-Government and the Supreme Court in *R.* v. *Pamajewon*" (1997) 42 *McGill L.J.* 1011; J. Borrows, "Creating Indigenous Legal Community" (2005) 50 *McGill L. J.* 153; R. Neizen, "Culture and the Judiciary: The Meaning of the Culture Concept as a Source of Aboriginal Rights in Canada" (2003) 2 *Can. J. L. & Soc'y* 1.

43 Canada, British Columbia, & Nisga'a Nation, *Nisga'a Final Agreement & Appendices*; www.gov.bc.ca/arr/firstnation/nisgaa/default.html# Ch. 8, s. 9 [hereinafter NFA].

44 *Ibid.* Ch. 8, s. 4.

45 *Ibid.* Ch. 8, s. 7 a.

46 *Ibid.* Ch. 8, s. 7 b.

47 July 22, 2005 interview in Vancouver, BC.

48 *R.* v. *Pamajewon,* [1996] 2 S.C.R. 821.

49 *Criminal Code,* R.S.C., 1985, c. C-46.

50 *Supra* note 48 at para. 24.

51 *Supra* note 33 at para 56.

52 *Supra* note 48 at para. 27.

53 *Ibid.* at para. 28.

54 *R.* v. *Gardner* (1994), 21 O.R. (3d) 385 at 400, quoted in *Pamajewon, supra* note 48 at para. 29.

55 See M. C. Lazarus, E. D. Morzon & R. B. Wodnicki, "The Mohawks of Kahnawa:ke and the case for an Aboriginal Right to Gaming under the Constitution Act 1982" (2006) *Gaming L. Rev.* 369.

56 *Supra* note 4 at 125–26.

57 *Manitoba Act, 1870.* 33 Victoria, c 3.

58 *Supra* note 4 at 121.

59 P. Macklem, "Normative Dimensions of an Aboriginal Right of Self-Government" (1995–96) *21 Queen's L.J.* 173 at 213.

60 See *Delgamuukw* v. *British Columbia* (1997) 3 S.C.R. 1010 (S.C.C.). This case is the most authoritative on the general characterization of Aboriginal rights, though the precise legal working out of self-government rights is not attempted.

61 For examples of Aboriginal and treaty rights cases, see *R.* v. *Badger* [1996] 1 S.C.R. 771; *R.* v. *Gladstone* [1996] 2 S.C.R. 723; *R.* v. *N.T.C. Smokehouse Ltd.,* [1996] 2 S.C.R. 672; *R.* v. *Marshall* [1999] 3 S.C.R. 456; *R.* v. *Marshall* [1999] 3 S.C.R. 533; *R.* v. *Marshall* [2005] SCC 3006; and *R.* v. *Sparrow* [1990] 1 S.C.R. 1075.

62 E. Metcalfe, "Illiberal Citizenship? A Critique of Will Kymlicka's Liberal Theory of Minority Rights" (1996–97) 22 *Queen's L. J.* 167 at 206.

63 P. Macklem, "Distributing Sovereignty: Indian Nations and Equality of Peoples" (1992-3) 45 *Stan. L. Rev.* 1131 at 1355.

64 R. Spaulding, "People as National Minorities: A Review of Will Kymlicka's Arguments for Aboriginal Rights from a Self-Determination Perspective" (1997) 47 *University of Toronto L. J.* 35 at 48–54.

65 Kymlicka, *supra* note 4 at 120.

66 *Ibid.* at 120.

67 *Ibid.* at 152.

68 *Ibid.* at 153.

69 *Ibid.* at 171.

70 D. Turner, *This is not a Peace Pipe: Towards a Critical Indigenous Philosophy* (Toronto: University of Toronto Press, 2006) at 70.

71 M. Foucault, *The Archaeology of Knowledge*, Trans. A. M. Sheridan (London: Routledge, 1972).

72 *Ibid*; M. Foucault, *Society Must be Defended*, Trans. D. Macey (London: Penguin, 2003); M. Foucault, *The Will to Knowledge: The History of Sexuality 1*, Trans. R. Hurley (London: Penguin, 1976); M. Foucault, *The Birth of the Clinic: An Archeology of Medical Perception*, Trans. A. M. Sheridan-Smith (London: Tavistock, 1970.); and M. Foucault, *Madness and Civilization: A History of Insanity in the Age of Reason*, Trans. R. Howard (London: Tavistock, 1965).

73 R. Young, *Postcolonialism: A Historical Introduction* (Oxford: Blackwell, 2001) at 400.

74 *Ibid.* at 410.

75 *Supra* note 6 at 103.

76 *Ibid.* at 171.

77 *Ibid.* at 3.

78 *Ibid.*

79 *Supra* note 33 at para 91.

80 *Ibid.* at para 50.

81 *Supra* note 6 at 3.

82 *Ibid.* at 51.

83 *Society Must be Defended, supra* note 72 at 95.

84 *Ibid.*

Notes to Chapter 2

1   *Constitution Act, 1982* (U.K.) 1982, c. 11. Section 35(1) reads, "The existing and aboriginal treaty rights of the aboriginal peoples of Canada are hereby recognized and affirmed."

2   D. Turner, *This is not a Peace Pipe: Towards a Critical Indigenous Philosophy* (Toronto: University of Toronto Press, 2006) at 5.

3   Canada, British Columbia, & Nisga'a Nation, *Nisga'a Final Agreement & Appendices*; www.gov.bc.ca/arr/firstnation/nisgaa/default.html#.

4   *Act Against Slavery* (1793) 33 Geo. III, c.7 (U.C.).

5   See D. Raunet, *Without Surrender, Without Consent: A History of the Nisga'a Land Claims* (Vancouver: Douglas & McIntyre, 1996) at 21.

6   G. P. V. Akrigg & H. B. Akrigg, *British Columbia Chronicle, 1778–1846* (Vancouver: Discovery Press, 1975) at 94.

7   *Supra* note 5 at 22.

8   *Ibid.* at 17.

9   *Ibid.* at 25.

10 *Ibid.* at 25.

11 See A. Twigg, *Thompson's Highway: British Columbia's Fur Trade: 1800-1850* (Vancouver: Ronsdale Press, 2006). This is a collection of biographies of individuals engaged in the early fur trade.

12 *Supra* note 5 at 26–29.

13 *Royal Proclamation, 1763,* (U.K.), 14 Geo. III, c.83.

14 See J. L. Tobias, "Protection, Civilization, Assimilation: An Outline History of Canada's Indian Policy," in I. A. L. Getty & A. S. Lussier (Eds.), *As Long as the Sun Shines and Water Flows: A Reader in Canadian Native Studies* (Vancouver: UBC Press, 1983) at 40.

15 See *Delgamuukw* v. *British Columbia* [1991] 3 W.W.R. 97, 79 D.L.R. (4th) 185, [1991] 5 C.N.L.R. 1. (B.C.S.C.). Justice McEachern describes the refusal of the British government to provide funds for the negotiation of treaties with the Aboriginal groups that had not yet entered into treaties at para. 793-801.

16 Cited in Raunet, *supra* note 5 at 91.

17 See Nisga'a Tribal Council, *Ayuukhl Nisga'a Study: Nisga'a Society,* Vol. III (New Aiyansh: Wilp Wilxo'oskwhl Nisga'a Publications, 1995); and Nisga'a Tribal Council, *Ayuukhl Nisga'a Study: Nisga'a Clan Histories,* Vol. II (New Aiyansh: Wilp Wilxo'oskwhl Nisga'a Publications, 1995).

18 F. Cassidy, "Self-Determination, Sovereignty, and Self-Government," in F. Cassidy (Ed.), *Aboriginal Self-Determination* (Lantzville/Halifax: Oolichan/The Institute for Research on Public Policy, 1991) at 7.

19 Nisga'a Tribal Council, *Ayuukhl Nisga'a Study: The Land and Resources,* Vol. IV (New Aiyansh: Wilp Wilxo'oskwhl Nisga'a Publications, 1995) at 18.

20 Nisga'a Nation, *Lock Stock and Barrel: Nisga'a Ownership Statement* (New Aiyansh: Nisga'a Lisims Government) at 88.

21 *Supra* note 5 at 136.

22 *Ibid.* at 83. This word translates in English as "Get off my land."

23 *Ibid.* at xiv.

24 Interview with Eric Grandison in New Aiyansh, July 12, 2005.

25 British Columbia, *The Nishga petition to His Majesty's Privy Council [microform]: a record of interviews with the government of Canada together with related documents* (Conference of Friends of the Indians of British Columbia: Witness Press, 1915) at 1-2.

26 *Ibid.* at 11–12; "Mr. Scott's Memorandum, Department of Indian Affairs, Canada, Ottawa, March 11, 1914."

27 *St. Catherine's Milling and Lumber Co. v. R.,* (1889) 2 C.N.L.C. 541 (J.C.P.C.).

28 *Ibid.* at 549.

29 *Indian Act,* R.S.C., 1985 c. 1–5. This legislation originally enacted in 1876 regulated the status and entitlement of persons defined as Indians. This statute has since this time governed almost every aspect of Aboriginal people's lives through the government Indian administration (Department of Indian and Northern Affairs).

30 *Supra* note 5 at 142.

31 *Ibid.* at 129.

32 *Ibid.* at 146.

33 *Calder v. A.G.* [1973] 4 W.W.R. 1 (S.C.C.).

34 *Supra* note 13.

35   Canada, Indian Affairs and Northern Development, *Statement of the First Government of Canada on Indian Policy, 1969; presented to the first session of the twenty-eighth Parliament by Honourable Jean Chrétien; Minister of Indian Affairs and Northern Development* (Ottawa: Queen's Printer, 1969) [hereinafter the *White Paper*].

36   See H. Cardinal, *The Unjust Society* (Edmonton: Hurtig, 1969).

37   Bhabha, H. K. *The Location of Culture* (London: Routledge, 1994) at 54.

38   *Supra* note 5 at 161.

39   *The James Bay and Northern Quebec Agreement*; www.gcc.ca/pdf/LEG00000006.pdf.

40   *Kanatewat* v. *James Bay Development Corp., Kanatewat* v. *Quebec Hydro Electric Co.*, leave to appeal to SCC refused (1973), 41 DLR (3d) 1, (1975) CA 166, rev'g (1974) RP 38 (Que. SC).

41   See P. Rynard, "Welcome In, But Check Your Rights at the Door": The James Bay and Nisga'a Agreements in Canada" (2000) 33 *Canadian Journal of Political Science*, 211–243; M. Coon Come, "Survival in the Context of Mega-Resource Development: Experiences of the James Bay Crees and the First Nations of Canada," in M. Blaser, H. A. Feit & Glenn McRae (Eds.), *In the Way of Development: Indigenous Peoples, Life Projects and Globalization* (London: Zeds, 2004) 153–165; and B. Crank, "The Importance of Working Together: Exclusions, Conflicts and Participation in James Bay, Quebec," in M. Blaser, H. A. Feit & Glenn McRae (Eds.), *In the Way of Development: Indigenous Peoples, Life Projects and Globalization* (London: Zed s, 2004) 166–186.

42   *Canada Act, 1982* (U.K.) 1982, c. 11, s. 35.

43   B.C. Treaty Commission website; www.bctreaty.net/. The BC Treaty Commission was founded in 1992.

44   See *Delgamuukw* v. *British Columbia* [1997] 3 S.C.R. 1010. (S.C.C.).

45   *Supra* note 3, Ch. 11, s.33.

46   Interview with Kevin McKay in New Aiyansh, held on July 13, 2005.

47   T. Molloy, *The World is Our Witness: The Historic Journey of the Nisga'a into Canada* (Calgary: Fifth House, 2000) at 123.

48   *Ibid.*

49   *Ibid.* at 124.

50   *Supra* note 3, Ch. 3, s. 3.

51   *Supra* note 44 at para. 113.

52 *Supra* note 3 at Ch. 2.

53 *Hofer* v. *Hofer* [1970] S.C.R. 958.

54 W. Kymlicka, *Multicultural Citizenship: A Liberal Theory if Minority Rights* (Oxford: Clarendon Press, 1995) at 161.

55 J. Borrows, "Wampum at Niagara: The Royal Proclamation, Canadian Legal History, and Self-Government," in M. Asch (Ed.), *Aboriginal and Treaty Rights in Canada: Essays on Law, Equality and Respect for Difference* (Vancouver: UBC Press, 1997) 427 at 161.

56 S. Harring, *White Man's Law: Native Peoples in Nineteenth Century Canadian Jurisprudence* (Toronto: Osgoode Society for Canadian Legal History, 1988).

57 See P. Rynard, *supra* note 41. See also, Rynard, "The Nisga'a Treaty: Are we on the Right Track?" (2004) 11 *International Journal on Minority and Group Rights* 289-298.

58 *Supra* note 3, Ch 3, s.4 (a).

59 *Ibid.,* Ch.3, s. 5.

60 *Mabo and Others* v. *Queensland (No. 2)* [1992] HCA 23; (1992) 175 CLR at para. 45.

61 *Supra* note 3, Ch. 3 s. 7.

62 See M. Asch & N. Zlotkin, "Affirming Aboriginal Title: A New Basis for Comprehensive Land Claims," in M. Asch (Ed.) *Aboriginal and Treaty Rights: Essays in Law, Equality and Respect for Difference* (Vancouver: UBC Press, 1997).

63 Rynard, *supra* note 41 at 241.

64 *Ibid.* at 225.

65 *Supra* note 5 at 170–71.

66 See H. de Soto, *The Mystery of Capital: Why Capitalism Triumphs in the West and Fails Everywhere Else* (New York: Random House, 2000).

67 Interview in Gitwinksihlkw, July 13, 2005.

68 *Supra* note 37 at 171.

69 *Supra* note 26.

70 *Supra* note 37 at 161.

71 *Ibid.*

72 *Ibid.* at 153.

73 *Ibid.* at 172.

74 *Supra* note 37 at 161.

75 *Ibid.* at 153.

76 Interview at New Aiyansh, July 12, 2005.

77 *Ibid.*

78 *Ibid.*

79 Rynard, *supra* note 41 at 211.

Notes to Chapter 3

1   Canada, British Columbia, & Nisga'a Nation, *Nisga'a Final Agreement & Appendices*; www.gov.bc.ca/arr/firstnation/nisgaa/default.html#, Ch. 5, s. 3 & 4.

2   D. Dukelow, *Dictionary of Canadian Law* 3rd ed. (Toronto: Carswell, 2002) at 295.

3   T. W. Merrill, "Property and the Right to Exclude" (1998) 77 *Neb L. Rev.* 730–39 at 730.

4   D. Raunet, *Without Surrender, Without Consent: A History of the Nisga'a Land Claims* (Vancouver: Douglas & McIntyre, 1996) at 181.

5   *Ibid.* at 185.

6   *Supra* note 1, Ch. 5, s. 6.

7   *Ibid.,* s. 8.

8   *Ibid.* s. 9.

9   *Ibid.* s. 10.

10 *Ibid.* s. 11.

11 *Ibid.* s. 12

12 *Ibid.* s. 10.

13 *Woodlot Licence Planning and Practices Regulation* [B.C. Reg. 21/2004]; www.for.gov.bc.ca/tasb/legsregs/frpa/frparegs/woodlotlicplanprac/ wlppr.htm#section14.

14 www.for.gov.bc.ca/hcp/fia/landbase/MoFIPPControlStandards.pdf.

15 *Supra* note 1, Ch. 5, s. 9.

16 *Ibid.,* s. 10.

17 Nisga'a Tribal Council, *Ayuukhl Nisga'a Study: The Land and Resources*, Vol. IV (New Aiyansh: Wilp Wilxo'oskwhl Nisga'a Publications, 1995) at 77.

18 *Ibid.* at 43.

19 *Supra* note 1, Ch. 5, s. 58.

20 *Ibid.* at s. 59 & 60.

21 See chapter 4.

22 See *The Constitution Act, 1867*, 30 & 31 Victoria, c. 3. Section 91(24) provides that the federal government has jurisdiction over "Indians, and Lands reserved for the Indians."

23 S. Raimi (director), *Spiderman,* DVD (Sony Pictures, 2002).

24 *Supra* note 1, Ch 5. s. 32.

25 See P. Rynard, "'Welcome In, but Check Your Rights at the Door': The James Bay and Nisga'a Agreements in Canada" (2000) 33:2 *Canadian Journal of Political Science / Revue canadienne de science politique*, 211–43.

26 Interview at New Aiyansh, July 13, 2005.

27 *Supra* note 1, Ch. 5, s. 76.

28 *Forest Act.* [RSBC 1996] Ch. 157, s. 77.

29 *Supra* note 1, Ch. 5, s. 76-78.

30 *Supra* note 17 at 49.

31 *Van der Peet* v. R. [1996] 2 S.C.R. 507.

32 D. Harris, *Fish, Law and Colonialism: The Legal Capture of Salmon in British Columbia* (Toronto: University of Toronto Press, 2001) at 214.

33 *Ibid.* at 4.

34 *Supra* note 1, Ch. 8, s. 1.

35 *Ibid.* at s. 1(a).

36 *Ibid.* at s. 1(b).

37 See Fisheries and Oceans Canada, "A Recent Account of Canada's Atlantic Cod Fishery"; www.dfo-mpo.gc.ca/kids-enfants/map-carte/map_e.htm. A moratorium on cod fishing was announced on July 2, 1992, in response to concerns about declining cod stocks.

38 *Supra* note 1, Ch. 8, s. 2.

39 A favourite way to eat oolichan grease is to slather it on salmon jerky.

40 *Supra* note 17 at 97.

41 *Ibid.* at 49.

42 See Royal B.C. Museum, "Introduction"; www.livinglandscapes.bc.ca/north-west/oolichan_history/fishery_bay.htm.

43 *Supra* note 1, Ch. 8, s. 62 & 63.

44 *Ibid.* at s. 68.

45 *Ibid.* at s. 99 (a)-(c).

46 *Ibid.* at s. 115.

47 Sierra Club, "Nass Salmon Fishery gets Top Marks" (Aug. 9, 2006); www.sierraclub.bc.ca/quick-links/media-centre/media-releases/nass-salmon-fishery-gets-top-marks. See also, D. Levy, *Nass River Salmon Fishery: Report Card* (Sierra Club: August, 2006); www.sierraclub.ca/national/postings/scc-nass-salmon-report-card.pdf.

48 *Ibid.*

49 *Supra* note 1, Ch. 8, s. 111.

50 *Ibid.* at Ch. 9, s. 1.

51 *Ibid.* at s. 2.

52 *Ibid.* at s. 5.

53 *Ibid.* at s. 10.

54 *Ibid.* at s. 4.

55 *Ibid.* at s. 15.

56 *Ibid.* at s. 18.

57 *Ibid.* at s. 21.

58 *Ibid.* at s. 22.

59 *Ibid.* at s. 37.

60 *Ibid.* at s. 37(a)-(g).

61 *Ibid.* at s. 41.

62 *Ibid.* at s. 70 & 92.

63 *Ibid.* at s. 93.

64 *Supra* note 17 at 43.

65 Ministry of Environment, B.C. Government, "*The Wildlife Act*: Managing for Sustainability in the 21st Century," Discussion Paper (March 2007) at 27; www.env.gov.bc.ca/fw/wildlifeactreview/discussion/disc_08.html.

66 *Ibid.* at 25–26.

67 *Supra* note 1, Ch. 9, s. 77.

68 *Ibid.* at Chapter 1, Definitions.

69 *Ibid.* at Ch. 3, s. 20.

70 *Ibid.* at Ch. 3, s. 57–59.

71 *Supra* note 31 at para 43.

72 See *Delgamuukw* v. *British Columbia*, [1991] 3 W.W.R. 97, 79 D.L.R. (4th) 185, [1991] 5 C.N.L.R. 1. (B.C.S.C.).

73 *Supra* note 25 at 212.

74 *Ibid.*

75 *Ibid.* at 241.

76 P. Macklem, "First Nations Self-Government and the Borders of the Canadian Legal Imagination" (1991) 36 *McGill L. J.* 382–456.

77 *Ibid. at* 391–395.

Notes to Chapter 4

1 See chapter 1 for discussion of self-government in the *Penner Report* and *RCAP.*

2 "Alberta First Nations Take Legal Stand on Oil Sands"; www.tarsandswatch.org/alberta-first-nations-take-legal-stand-oil-sands.

3 R. Prokhovnik, *Sovereignties: Contemporary Theory and Practice* (Baskingstoke: Palgrave Macmillan, 2007) at 14.

4 A. Benoist, "What is Sovereignty" (1999) *Telos*, 99–118 at 99.

5 T. Hobbes, *Leviathan* (Peterborough: Broadview, 2002) at 128.

6 *Ibid.* at 129.

7 *Ibid.* at 93.

8 *Ibid.* at 95.

9 J. Bodin, *The Six Books of the Commonwealth* (Oxford: Blackwell, 1967), II, 2.

10 *Supra* note 4 at 102.

11 See R. Prokhovnik, *Sovereignty: History and Theory* (Exeter: Imprint Academic, 2008) at 79.

12 *Ibid.*

13 D. Ivison, *Postcolonial Liberalism* (Cambridge: Cambridge University Press, 2002) at 45.

14 See J. J. Rousseau, *A Discourse on the Origin of Inequality Among Men* (1754).

15 *Supra* note 11 at 98.

16 *Ibid.* at 101.

17 See C. Schmitt, *Political Theology: Four Chapters on the Concept of Sovereignty* (Cambridge MA: The MIT Press, 1986) at 1.

18 *Ibid.* at 6.

19 *Emergencies Act, 1985,* c. 22 (4th Supp.) .

20 G. Erasmus & J. Sanders, "Canadian History: An Aboriginal Perspective" in D. Englestad & J. Bird (eds.) *Nation to Nation: Aboriginal Sovereignty and the Future of Canada* (Concord: Anansi Press, 1992) 3–27 at 11.

21 Interview in New Aiyansh, July 13, 2005.

22 *Ibid.*

23 *Ibid.*

24 *Ibid.*

25 M. Asch, "Political Self-Sufficiency," in D. Englestad & J. Bird (Eds.), *Nation to Nation: Aboriginal Sovereignty and the Future of Canada* (Concord: Anansi Press, 1992) 45–52 at 50.

26 *Indian Act*, R.S.C., 1985, c. I-5.

27 Interview in New Aiyansh, July 12, 2005.

28 *Supra* note 21.

29 Canada, British Columbia and the Nisga'a Nation, *Nisga'a Final Agreement & Appendices*; www.gov.bc/arr/firstnation/nisgaa/default.html#, Ch. 2 s. 1.

30 H. K. Bhabha, *The Location of Culture* (London: Routledge, 1994) at 246.

31 *Ibid.* at 233.

32 W. Kymlicka, *Multicultural Citizenship: A Liberal Theory if Minority Rights* (Oxford: Clarendon Press, 1995) at 188.

33 *Supra* note 26.

34 Canada, British Columbia, & Nisga'a Nation, *Nisga'a Final Agreement & Appendices*; www.gov.bc.ca/arr/firstnation/nisgaa/default.html# Ch. 11, s. 6.

35 J. Borrows, *Recovering Canada: The Resurgence of Indigenous Law* (Toronto: University of Toronto Press, 2002) at 104–05.

36 *Constitution of the Nisga'a Nation* (New Aiyansh: Nisga'a Lisims Government, 1998) at s. 5(3).

37 Interview with Deanna Nyce in New Aiyansh, July 14, 2005.

38 *Supra* note 34, Ch. 11, s. 33.

39 *Ibid.* at s. 39.

40 *Supra* note 36 at 8(1).

41 *Ibid.* at 8(2).

42 *Supra* note 32 at 124.

43 *Ibid. at* 125–26.

44 J. Carpay, "Aboriginals in Canada: segregation or equality" C2C; www.c2cjournal.ca/public/articles/43.

45 *Supra* note 32 at 134–35.

46 See Migration Watch UK, "The Right of Non Citizens to Vote in Britain" (12 Feb., 2008); www.migrationwatchuk.com/Briefingpapers/legal/8_22_TheRight_ of_NonCitizensVoteBritain.asp. Commonwealth citizens have the right to vote in UK elections, though groups such as Migration Watch cite that "It devalues the concept of citizenship which the government is seeking to encourage," and wish voting to be restricted to UK citizens and those countries who have reciprocal voting rights.

47 See J. Hicks & G. White, "Nunavut: Inuit Self-Determination Through a Land Claim and Public Government," in J. Dahl, J. Hicks & P. Jull (Eds.), *Nunavut: Inuit regain control of their lands and their lives* (Copenhagen: International Work Group for Indigenous Affairs, 2000), 30-115; www.anu.edu.au/caepr/Publications/topical/HicksJ_WhiteG_2000.pdf.

48 *Supra* note 34, Ch. 11 s. 20.

49 *Supra* note 32 at 13.

50 *Ibid.* at 182.

51 Definition from Princeton, Wordnet; http://wordnet.princeton.edu/.

52 *Supra* note 34, Ch. 11 s. 78.

53 See *Reference re Same-Sex Marriage*, [2004] 3 S.C.R. 698.

54 *Marriage Act* B.C. [R.S.B.C. 1996] Ch. 282.

55 *Vital Statistics Act* [RSBC] Ch. 479.

56 *Supra* note 34, Ch. 11, s. 102.

57 R. Peacock, "District Review Report: School District No. 92 (Nisga'a), April 11-13" (Victoria: British Columbia, Ministry of Education and Nisga'a School District, 2005).

58 INAC, "House of Wisdom Draws the World"; www.ainc-inac.gc.ca/bc/fnbc/sucsty/suscom/ed/howisd_e.html.

59 "About Wilp Wilxo'oskwhl Nisga'a Institute"; http://wwni.bc.ca/about.htm.

60 http://wwni.bc.ca/mission.htm.

61 K. Burch, *"Property" and the Making of the International System* (London: Lynne Reiner Publishers, 1998) at 159.

62 *Supra* note 30 at 162.

63 H. K. Bhabha, "Introduction: Narrating the Nation" in H. K. Bhabha (Ed.), *Nation and Narration* (London: Routledge, 2001) at 1.

Notes to Chapter 5

1 Canada, British Columbia, & Nisga'a Nation, *Nisga'a Final Agreement & Appendices*; www.gov.bc.ca/arr/firstnation/nisgaa/default.html#.

2 *Campbell* v. *British Columbia (A.G.)* (2000) 8 W.W.R. 600; 189 D.L.R. (4th) 333 (B.C.S.C.).

3 *Chief Mountain* v. *British Columbia (Attorney General),* 2011 BCSC 1394 [hereinafter *Chief Mountain*].

4 T. Molloy, *The World is Our Witness: The Historic Journey of the Nisga'a into Canada* (Calgary: Fifth House, 2000) at 88.

5 *Ibid.* at 108.

6 *Supra* note 2 at para. 1.

7 *Ibid.* at para. 12.

8 The BC Legislature gave its assent on April 23, 1999. The last step needed to give legal effect to the treaty took place on April 13, 2000, when Parliament passed the Nisga'a Final Agreement Act. British Columbia "Nisga'a Final Agreement"; www.gov.bc.ca/arr/firstnation/nisgaa/default.html.

9 *A. G. Ontario* v. *A. G. Canada,* [1912] A.C. 571.

10 *Ibid.* at 581.

11 *Reference re Secession of Quebec,* [1998] 2 S.C.R. 217.

12 *Ibid.* at 244–45.

13 *Mitchell* v. *Peguis Indian Band* [1990] 2 S.C.R. 85 at p. 108–09.

14 *Ibid.* at para. 81.

15 *R.* v. *Van der Peet,* [1996] 2 S.C.R. 507.

16 *Ibid.* at para. 49.

17 See P. Fitzpatrick, "'We Know What It Is When You Do Not Ask Us': The Un-challengable Nation" (2004) *XV Finnish Yearbook of International Law,* 130.

18 *Supra* note 2 at para. 124.

19 *Ibid.* at para. 59.

20 *Ibid.* at para. 32.

21 *Ibid.* at para. 33.

22 J. R. Saul, *A Fair Country: Telling Truths About Canada* (Toronto: Penguin, 2008).

23 Métis are a self-identified cultural group who are of mixed European and Abo-riginal heritage.

24 www.octopusbooks.org/book/fair-country-telling-truths-about-canada.

25 P. Tuitt, *Race, Law and Resisance* (London: Glasshouse Press, 2004) at 89.

26 *re The Initiative and Referendum Act,* [1919] A.C. 935 (J.C.P.C.).

27 *Ibid.* at 945.

28 *Supra* note 2 at para. 149.

29 *Ibid.* at para. 150.

30 *Delgamuukw* v. *British Columbia,* 1991 CanLii 2327 at 495 (B.C.S.C.).

31 *Supra* note 2 (2000) 8 W.W.R. 601 at para. 151.

32 In 1996, then-Reform MP and current Liberal MP Keith Martin called it "apart-heid," saying in Parliament that "it creates different laws for different people. It is by definition racist"; www.westernstandard.ca/website/article.php?id=2726&start=1.

33 *Supra* note 2 at para. 152.

34 *Ibid.* at para. 155.

35 *Ibid.* at para. 158.

36 *Ibid.* at para. 179.

37 *Ibid.* at para. 181.

38 *Supra* note 25 at 89.

39 *Ibid.* at 77.

40 CBC News, "B.C. Liberals Drop Nisga'a Lawsuit" (Aug. 30, 2001); www.cbc.ca/canada/story/2001/08/30/bc_treaty010830.html.

41 *Ibid.*

42 CBC News, "B.C. Treaty Referendum" (July 2, 2004); www.cbc.ca/news/background/aboriginals/bc_treaty_referendum.html.

43 *Ibid.*

44 *Ibid.*

45 *Supra* note 3 at para. 38–39.

46 *Ibid.* at para. 19–20.

47 *Ibid.* at para. 236.

48 *Ibid.* at para. 287.

49 *Ibid.*

50 2010 SCC 53.

51 *Ibid.* at para. 54.

52 D. Ivison, "Decolonizing the Rule of Law: *Mabo*'s case as Postcolonial Constitutionalism" (1997) 17 *Oxford Journal of Legal Studies*: 2 at 273.

53 S. Motha, "Mabo: Encountering the Epistemic Limit of the Recognition of 'Difference'" (1998) 7 *Griffith Law Review* 79 at 95.

54 *Ibid.* at 88.

55 See P. Rynard, ""Welcome In, but Check Your Rights at the Door": The James Bay and Nisga'a Agreements in Canada" (2000) 33:2 *Canadian Journal of Political Science*, 211.

56 J. Carpay, "Aboriginals in Canada: Segregation or Equality," C2C; http://c2c-journal.ca/2009/06/aboriginals-in-canada-segregation-or-equality.

57 J. D. Weston, "National Implications of Chief Mountain's Challenge to the Third Order of Government and the Nisga'a Treaty." Presentation to the Fraser Institute, Vancouver, Feb. 19, 2003; www.reformbc.net/news2003/Feb19_03.pdf at p. 11.

58 *Supra* note 53 at 95.

59 J. Carpay, "An Appeal for Justice"; www.canadianconstitutionfoundation.ca/files/pdf/newsrelease-09-18-2006.pdf.

60 Canadianchristianity.com, "Comment: 'I am Canadian,' says Nisga'a treaty opponent"; www.canadianchristianity.com/cgi-bin/na.cgi?nationalupdates/040303 canadian.

61 *Supra* note 57.

62 H. K. Bhabha. *The Location of Culture* (London: Routledge, 1994) at 3.

63 H. Bhabha, "Interview," in F. Afzal-Khan & K. Seshadri-Crooks (Eds.), *The Pre-Occupation of Postcolonial Studies* (London: Duke University Press, 2000) at 373.

Notes to Chapter 6

1 As I write this, I am appreciating the irony of my automatic spellchecker capitalizing "european."

2 J. Y. Henderson, "Postcolonial Indigenous Legal Consciousness," 1 (2002) *Indigenous Law Journal* at 49.

3 *Canadian Charter of Rights and Freedoms,* Being *Schedule B* to the *Canada Act 1982* (U.K.) 1982, c. 11.

4 See BC Treaty Commission; www.bctreaty.net/.

5 See J. R. Saul, *A Fair Country: Telling Truths about Canada* (Toronto: Viking Canada, 2008).

6 See G. W. F. Hegel, *Phenomenology of Spirit.* Trans. A. V. Miller with analysis of the text and foreword by J. N. Findlay (Oxford: Clarendon Press, 1977), para. 179. Hegel argues that the master-slave dialectic is fundamental in the discovery of self-consciousness. I apologize if this is a simplification of this contentious and debated philosophical concept. For my purposes I merely mean to suggest that the Hegelian dialectic which requires a subjugation is not the best approach to inter-cultural relations.

7 J. Bird, "Introduction" in D. Englestad & J. Bird (Eds.), *Nation to Nation* (Concord: Anansi, 1992) at xix.

8 J. P. Sartre, *Colonialism and Neocolonialism* (London: Routledge, 2006) at 159.

9 www.nisgaalisims.ca/files/nlg/Nisga'a%20Landholding%20Transition%20Act%20(October%202009).pdf.

10 www.nisgaalisims.ca/node/99.

11 *R.* v. *Van der Peet,* [1996] 2 S.C.R. 507.

12 *R.* v. *Pamajewon,* [1996] 2 S.C.R. 821.

13 H. K. Bhabha, *The Location of Culture* (London: Routledge, 1994) at 3.

14 www.ushistory.org/declaration/document/index.htm.

15 See, for example, the *Treaty on European Union (Maastricht Treaty),* 1993, which established the European Union (EU).

16 P. Tuitt, *Race, Law and Resistance* (London: Glasshouse Press, 2004) at 89.

17 *Supra* note 5.

18 *Constitution Act, 1982* (U.K.) 1982, c. 11.

19 J. Ibbitson, W. Kymlicka, et al. (Eds.), *Uneasy Partners: Multiculturalism and Rights in Canada* (Wilfred Laurier University Press, 2007) at 50.

20 *Ibid.* at 57

21 *Indian Act,* R.S.C., 1985, c. I-5.

22 *The Report of the Royal Commission on Aboriginal Peoples*; www.collections-canada.gc.ca/webarchives/20071115053257/http://www.ainc-inac.gc.ca/ch/rcap/sg/sgmm_e.html. Recommendations at www.collectionscanada.gc.ca/webarchives/20071115053257/http://www.ainc-inac.gc.ca/ch/rcap/sg/sha6a_e.html at 2.3.45.

23 *Ibid.* at 2.3.46.

24 *Ibid.* at 2.3.48.

25 *Ibid.* at 2.3.50.

26 The Department of Indian Affairs and Northern Developments, or Indian and Northern Affairs Canada, has been renamed Aboriginal Affairs and Northern Development Canada, though there is no indication that the departmental structure has been altered in any significant way.

27 *Supra* note 22 at 2.3.50.

28 *Supra* note 2 at 13.

29 R. Young, "Preface," in J. P. Sartre, *Colonialism and Neocolonialism* (London: Routledge, 2006) at xv–xvi.

30 H. Cardinal, *The Unjust Society: The Tragedy of Canada's Indians* (Edmonton: Hurtig, 1969) at 64.

Glossary[*]

Ango'oskw — traditional hunting and gathering grounds.

Ayuuk Nisga'a — cultural law of the Nisga'a.

K'amligiihahlhat — the creator.

Nisga'a Lisims Government — the name of the central authority of the Nisga'a federal government. Nisga'a government is comprised of the Nisga'a Lisims Government, and the four Nisga'a Village Governments (Gitlaxt'aamiks, Gitwinksihlkw, Laxgalts'ap, and Gingolx).

Pdeek — tribe.

Wilp — 1) house; 2) extended maternal family.

Wilp Wilxo'oskwhl Nisga'a — Nisga'a post-secondary institution. The name translates to "Nisga'a House of Wisdom."

Simgigat — (plural) Nisga'a chiefs.

Sigidim haanak — (plural) Nisga'a matriarchs.

Wilp Si'ayuukhl Nisga'a — Nisga'a legislative house.

[*] Definitions are taken from *Nisga'a Dictionary*, 1st Ed. (New Aiyansh: WWN, 2001).

Selected Bibliography

Statutes, Treaties and Government Resources

Calder v. *A.G.* [1974] 4 W.W.R. 1 (B.C.S.C.).

Canada Act, 1982 (U.K.) 1982, c. 11.

Canada, Indian Affairs and Northern Development, *Statement of the First Government of Canada on Indian Policy, 1969 / presented to the first session of the twenty-eighth Parliament by Honourable Jean Crétien, Minister of Indian Affairs and Northern Development* (Ottawa: Queen's Printer, 1969).

Canada, British Columbia, & Nisga'a Nation, *Nisga'a Final Agreement & Appendices*; www.gov.bc.ca/arr/firstnation/nisgaa/default.html#.

House of Commons, *Special Committee on Indian Self-Government in Canada: Report of the Special Committee* ("Penner Report"), 1983.

Indian Act, R.S.C., 1985 c. 1-5.

Royal Proclamation, 1763 (U.K.), 14 Geo. III, c.83.

Cases

Calder v. *British Columbia*, (1973), 34 D.L.R. (3d) 145.

Campbell v. *British Columbia (A.G.)* (2000) 8 W.W.R. 600; 189 D.L.R. (4th) 333 (B.C.S.C.).

Delgamuukw v. *British Columbia*, [1991] 3 W.W.R. 97, 79 D.L.R. (4th) 185, [1991] 5 C.N.L.R. 1. (B.C.S.C.).

Delgamuukw v. *British Columbia*, [1997] 3 S.C.R. 1010.

Guerin v. *The Queen*, [1984] 2 S.C.R. 335.

House of Sga'Nisim v. *Canada* [2002] BCCA 362 (B.C.C.A.).

R. v. *Pamajewon*, [1996] 2 S.C.R. 821.

R. v. *St. Catherine's Milling and Lumber Co.*, (1889) 2 C.N.L.C. 541 (J.C.P.C.).

R. v. *Van der Peet*, [1996] 2 S.C.R. 507.

Articles

Barsh, R. L. & J. Y. Henderson, "The Supreme Court's *Van der Peet* Trilogy: Naïve Imperialism and Ropes of Sand" (1997) 42 *McGill L. J.* 994.

Benoist, A., "What is Sovereignty?" (1999) *Telos* 99-118.

Cassidy, F., "Self-Determination, Sovereignty, and Self-Government" in F. Cassidy (Ed.) *Aboriginal Self-Determination* (Lantzville/Halifax: Oolichan/The Institute for Research on Public Policy, 1991) 1–14.

Denis, C., "Indigenous Citizenship and History in Canada: Between Denial and Imposition," in R. Adamoski, D. Chunn, and R. Menzies (Eds.), *Contesting Canadian Citizenship. Historical Readings* (Peterborough: Broadview Press, 2002) 113–26.

Erasmus, D. & J. Sanders, "Canadian History: An Aboriginal Perspective," in D. Englestad & J. Bird (Eds.), *Nation to Nation: Aboriginal Sovereignty and the Future of Canada* (Concord: Anansi Press, 1992) 3–27.

Fitzpatrick, P., "'We Know What It Is When You Do Not Ask Us': The Unchallengable Nation," (2004) *Finnish Yearbook of International Law XV* 129.

Henderson, J. Y., "Postcolonial Indigenous Legal Consciousness" (2002) 1 *Indigenous Law Journal*.

Macklem, P., "Distributing Sovereignty: Indian Nations and Equality of Peoples" (1992-3) 45 *Stan. L. Rev.* 1311.

_____,"First Nations Self-Government and the Borders of the Canadian Legal Imagination" (1991) 36 *McGill L. J.* 382–456.

Metcalfe, E., "Illiberal Citizenship? A Critique of Will Kymlicka's Liberal Theory of Minority Rights" (1996–97) 22 *Queen's L. J.* 167.

Morse, B. W., "Permafrost Rights: Aboriginal Self-Government and the Supreme Court in *R. v. Pamajewon*" (1997) 42 *McGill L. J.* 1011.

Rynard, P., "'Welcome In, But Check Your Rights at the Door': The James Bay and Nisga'a Agreements in Canada" (2000) 33 *Canadian Journal of Political Science*, 211–43.

Spaulding, R., "People as National Minorities: A Review of Will Kymlicka's Arguments for Aboriginal Rights from a Self-Determination Perspective" (1997) 47 *University of Toronto L.J.* 35.

Tobias, J. L., "Protection, Civilization, Assimilation: An Outline History of Canada's Indian Policy" in I. A. L. Getty & A. S. Lussier (Eds.) *As Long as the Sun Shines and Water Flows: A Reader in Canadian Native Studies* (Vancover: UBC Press, 1983) 39–55.

Monographs

Akrigg, G. P. V. & H. B. Akrigg, *British Columbia Chronicle, 1778-1846* (Vancouver: Discovery Press, 1975).

Atleo, E. R., *Tsawalk: A Nuu-chah-nulth Worldview* (Vancouver: UBC Press, 2004).

Bhabha, H. K., *The Location of Culture* (London: Routledge, 1994).

Borrows, J., *Recovering Canada: The Resurgence of Indigenous Law* (Toronto: University of Toronto Press, 2002).

Cardinal, H., *The Unjust Society* (Edmonton: M. G. Hurtig Ltd, 1969).

de Soto, H., *The Mystery of Capital: Why Capitalism Triumphs in the West and Fails Everywhere Else* (New York: Random House, 2000).

Foucault, M., *The Archaeology of Knowledge*, Trans. A. M. Sheridan (London: Routledge, 1972).

_____, *Society Must be Defended*, Trans. D. Macey (London: Penguin, 2003).

_____, *The Will to Knowledge: The History of Sexuality 1*, Trans. R. Hurley (London: Penguin, 1976).

_____, *The Birth of the Clinic: An Archeology of Medical Perception*, Trans. A. M. Sheridan-Smith (London: Tavistock, 1970).

_____, *Madness and Civilization: A History of Insanity in the Age of Reason*, Trans. R. Howard (London: Tavistock, 1965).

Hobbes, T., *Leviathan* (Peterborough: Broadview, 2002).

Ivison, D., *Postcolonial Liberalism* (Cambridge: Cambridge University Press, 2002).

Ibbitson, J. & W. Kymlicka et al. (Eds.), *Uneasy Partners: Multiculturalism and Rights in Canada* (Wilfred Laurier University Press, 2007).

Kymlicka, W., *Liberalism, Community and Culture* (Oxford: Clarendon Press, 1989).

Kymlicka, W., *Multicultural Citizenship: A Liberal Theory if Minority Rights* (Oxford: Clarendon Press, 1995).

Molloy, T. with Donald Ward, *The World is Our Witness: The Historic Journey of the Nisga'a into Canada* (Calgary: Fifth House, 2000).

Nisga'a Tribal Council, *Ayuukhl Nisga'a Study: Nisga'a Clan Histories, Vol. I* (New Aiyansh: Wilp Wilxo'oskwhl Nisga'a Publications, 1995).

_____, *Ayuukhl Nisga'a Study: Nisga'a Clan Histories, Vol. II* (New Aiyansh: Wilp Wilxo'oskwhl Nisga'a Publlications, 1995).

Nisga'a Tribal Council, *Ayuukhl Nisga'a Study: Nisga'a Society, Vol. III* (New Aiyansh: Wilp Wilxo'oskwhl Nisga'a Publlications, 1995).

_____, *Ayuukhl Nisga'a Study: The Land and Resources, Vol. IV* (New Aiyansh: Wilp Wilxo'oskwhl Nisga'a Publlications, 1995).

Raunet, D., *Without Surrender, Without Consent: A History of the Nisga'a Land Claims* (Vancouver: Douglas & McIntyre, 1996).

Said, E. W., *Orientalism: Western Representations of the Orient* (Harmondsworth: Penguin, 1978).

Saul, J. R., *A Fair Country: Telling Truths About Canada* (Toronto: Penguin, 2008).

Sartre, J. P., *Colonialism and Neocolonialism* (London: Routledge, 2006) at 159.

Schmitt, C., *Political Theology: Four Chapters on the Concept of Sovereignty* (Cambridge MA: The MIT Press, 1986).

Tuitt, P., *Race, Law and Resisance* (London: Glasshouse Press, 2004).

Turner, D., *This is not a Peace Pipe: Towards a Critical Indigenous Philosophy* (Toronto: University of Toronto Press, 2006).

Young, R., *Postcolonialism: A Historical Introduction* (Oxford: Blackwell, 2001).

Online Resources

Aboriginal Affairs and Northern Development Canada, "General Briefing Note on Canada's Self-Government and Land Claims Policies and the Status of Negotiations January 2011"; www.ainc-inac.gc.ca/al/ldc/ccl/pubs/gbn/gbn-eng.asp#section1.

The Report of the Royal Commission on Aboriginal Peoples; www.collectionscanada. gc.ca/webarchives/20071115053257/http://www.ainc-inac.gc.ca/ch/rcap/sg/ sgmm_e.html.

Weston, J. "National Implications of Chief Mountain's Challenge to the Third Order of Government and the Nisga'a Treaty"; www.reformbc.net/news2003/ Feb19_03.pdf.

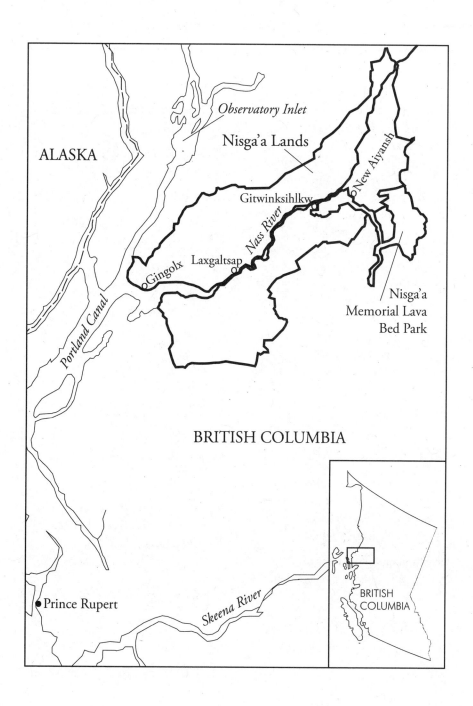

ALASKA

Observatory Inlet

Nisga'a Lands

New Aiyansh

Gitwinksihlkw

Nass River

Gingolx

Laxgaltsap

Nisga'a
Memorial Lava
Bed Park

Portland Canal

BRITISH COLUMBIA

Prince Rupert

Skeena River

BRITISH
COLUMBIA

Index

Calder, Frank 11, 54

Calder 12

Campbell, Gordon 117, 126–28

Campbell 16, 116, 117–26, 128, 129–30, 131, 133, 135, 142

Canadian Charter of Rights and Freedoms 25, 31, 138; entrenched 94; Nisga'a institutions subject to 56, 99–101, 128–29; not to "abrogate or derogate" 98, 99, 124; violated by NFA 118–20, 123–25, 128–29; sect.3 (voting rights) 118–19, 123–24; sect.7 128; sect.15 31, 128; sect.25 25, 101

Canadian sovereignty 14, 15, 96, 119, 122, 125, 135; extinguished claim for First Nation self-government 120–21; as product both Aboriginal and Canadian law 115, 117, 135

Cardinal, Harold 11, 16, 55, 139; The Red Paper 11–12, 16, 55, 146–47

Carpay, John 106, 132–33

Charlottetown Accord, 12

Chief Mountain 104, 128, 132, 133, 134–35, 136

Chief Mountain 106, 116, 126–35, 142

Chrétien, Jean 11-14, White Paper, *which see.*

citizenship: Canadian 11, 29, 100, 105, 128, 134, 143; definition 105–06; differentiated 14, 109, 124; ethnicity-based citizenship 106–09, 137, 144; layered 107–08; marriage and 105–06; Nisga'a 104–09, 114–15, 128. *See also* membership

"citizens plus" 108, 111

civil disobedience 64

collateral: land as 62, 140

colonial splitting 39

colonialism 18, 33–34, 37–39, 78, 110, 133, 139

Columbrander, Peter 10, 28

commercial fishing 10, 26, 40, 77–78, 79–82

commercialization of Nisga'a Lands 61–62, 77, 79, 81–82, 87, 127

common law principles 84

communal: rights 124; tenure 63

Constitution Act, 1867 118–19, 130

Constitution Act, 1982 sect.25 25, 98–99, 101; sect.35 12, 19, 25, 28–29, 98–99, 120, 122–25, 129, 143; sect.55 119, 122–23; sect.91&92 94–95, 118–19, 124, 129–30; sect.96 130; notwithstanding clause, *which see*

Constitution: as exhaustive inventory of law-making power in Canada 119–20, 122, 124; repatriation of 12. *See also* sovereignty: source of

constitutional conferences 13, 139

contact: early contact 11, 45–48, 53–54; problems associated with 47. *See also* Aboriginal culture: before contact; reconciliation; title

Cornwall, Clement 48

Criminal Code 28–29

Crown Proceedings Act, 1960 54

cultural diversity 119–20, 144; value of 30–31, 33

culture. *See* Aboriginal culture

de Soto, H 62

decision-making authority 95–98, 103–04, 109–14; governmental authority: limitations 31, 87, 98, 101–02, 120, 123–25

decolonization 16, 78, 91, 117, 132

Delgamuukw: recognized pre-existing Aboriginal title 12–14, 123; three aspects of sui generis Aboriginal title 58, 63; Supreme Court guidelines 10, 126

Denis, Claude 11

Department of Indian Affairs 52, 62

Department of Indian Affairs and Northern Development (DIAND) 144–45

designated species 82–83

Dickson, Chief Justice 120

difference: Aboriginal 132, 133, 136; cultural 18, 23–24, 40, 64, 99–101, 114–15, 136; "native difference" 88–89. *See also* test

discourse 19–20, 28, 34–35, 38, 42, 97–100, 123, 126, 133, 137 colonial 19, 37–39, 64; as making history 19, 36–37, 56, 88, 139; not unidirectional 37, 38–39, 42–43. *See also* language

Douglas, James 47–48

duty to consult 90, 130

Eagle Lake First Nation 28, 40

economy 67–68, 82; and culture 8m 10–11, 22, 26–27, 29, 40–50, 84–95, 126, 138, 140–41, 146; development of 28, 40, 46, 62–63; sustainable 10, 62, 66, 69, 80

education 59, 95, 138; NLG jurisdiction over 91, 109–14; post-secondary 112–14

Emergencies Act 94

employment opportunities 74–75, 76, 128

encroachment 45–49, 50

entitlements: fish 27, 78–80; wildlife 82–83, 84

enunciation 37–38, 41, 55, 115

equality 22–23, 25, 98–99, 107; justification 22–24, 31–33, 140; liberal 14, 18, 31–35, 108–09, 137–38; perception of 11–12, 14, 19, 143

escheat 44, 60–61

ethnicity-based rights 21–23, 35, 128, 133, 135–36; citizenship 106–09, 137, 144; polyethnic rights 21, 22–23; equality argument for 23, 31

evidentiary burden 13

extinction 37, 41, 67

fee simple and Nisga'a land ownership 44–45, 57–63, 83, 140

Tracie Lea Scott grew up in Hythe, a small town in Northern Alberta. After graduating high school she completed her Bachelors degree in English and History at the University of Alberta. Tracie completed her LLB in 2002. After receiving a scholarship, she continued on to the LLM program where, under the supervision of Bruce Ziff, she wrote a dissertation entitled "The Indian, the Law and the Land: An Analysis of the *Chippewas of Sarnia* Case Using P. W. Kahn's Cultural Approach to the Rule of Law," examining the legal anxiety around Aboriginal land claims in the *Chippewas of Sarnia* case. After successfully defending, she accepted an Overseas Research Scholarship to do her PhD at Birkbeck College, University of London.

While studying for her PhD, she was a member of the British Association for Canadian Studies, acting as graduate student representative for several years. She also worked as a policy official for the Ministry of Justice in 2008–09, where she supported the Perpetuities and Accumulations Bill through Parliament. The author successfully defended her dissertation entitled, "The Meaning of Sovereignty in a Multinational State: The Implications of a Postcolonial Legal Analysis of the Nisga'a Final Agreement." After completing her PhD, she returned to Edmonton to article with the Department of Justice, Canada. The author is now continuing her research into cross-cultural legal studies in the United Arab Emirates.